I0527904

IN THE GARDEN
OF THE BELOVED

IN THE GARDEN OF THE BELOVED

Reflections from a Simple Man's Spiritual Journey

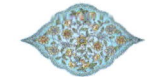

یک مرد ساده
A Simple Man

Tavern Publications
ENCINITAS, CALIFORNIA

Tavern Publications
Encinitas, California

10 9 8 7 6 5 4 3 2
First Edition 2023
Printed in the United States of America

ISBN: 979-8-218-24274-9
Library of Congress PCN Number: 2023913605

Book design by Dynamic Book Design
www.DynamicBookDesign.com

From Hafez:

The great religions are ships,
Poets are lifeboats,
Every sane person I know has jumped overboard.

From Ibn Arabi:

I profess the religion of Love,
Wherever its caravan turns along the way,
That is the belief, the faith I keep.

From Farid ud-Din Attar:

I know Nothing,
I understand Nothing,
I am unaware of Myself,
I am in Love,
But with whom I do not know.

From Rumi:

I do not know who I am.
I am in astounded, lucid confusion.

From Rumi:

Come, we know a way from the seen to the Unseen,
A path from the house you've lived in for so long,
To a garden that will take your breath away.

I've created this book for Friends who have asked

for a hardcopy of my poems, who love the feel

of a "real" book, with pages turned slowly by hand.

Within

Preface

The poems in this book are reflections from my life experience, described in depth in a companion volume, *An Affair of The Heart; a Spiritual Autobiography*[1]. These poems are not creative writing born of imagination, but expressions of direct experience.

I don't think of myself as a poet, or of the writings in this book as poetry. Rather, what's written here is prose, meted out slowly, comma-delineated, so that each phrase has an opportunity to sink from eye to mind to Heart. I had planned to explain the meanings of the metaphors and imagery I use, but was dissuaded by friends who, in their own initial readings, had no such knowledge, and applied meanings native to their own Heart and relationship with The Great Mystery.

The "poems" within were written with only one purpose; to Brighten; to Brighten hope in the Hearts of those in whom The Inner Radiance at the Heart of their Being is not yet aglow; to Brighten and hopefully Ignite the Ember within Hearts in which it flickers tenuously, and to Brighten the Flame in Hearts already Aglow in the Light of the Soul, the Atman, the Self; whatever one chooses to call

---

[1] In paperback and Kindle from Amazon; and online at https://GardenOfTheBeloved.com/
An_Affair_of_the_Heart/index.html.

our Essence. My hope for you is that these poems are not merely pleasant, uplifting words on a page, however inspiring, but are imbued with The Fragrance of that which is written of; that which calls to each of us from our deepest interiority.

Poems

The great religions are ships,
Poets are lifeboats,
Every sane person I know,
Has jumped overboard.

-Hafez

TOO DRUNK TO DREAM OF MORE

I've read that the goal of this life,
Is to reach Union with the Divine,
Forsaking this world of separation,
And abiding Eternally in Her arms.

But I have Vanished in that Embrace,
The Heaven of Nonexistent Existence,
Only to find, upon the world's return,
That I Loved creation more than ever.

For The Beautiful One followed me,
From the Kingdom of Heaven,
A stowaway in the Heart of my Being,
When the world, and I, returned.

I find myself now, ever confounded,
For I am individuated, but not separated,
Blessed by Her Perfect Residence,
In this residence, most imperfect.

How can I long for Heaven, there, then,
When She Holds me, here, now,
And Resting in Her arms, I swoon,
Too Drunk to dream of more.

AM I NOT HERE?

When I would sit to "meditate",
When I would strive to *do*,
Or refrain from doing,
The Beloved would whisper…

What are you doing?
Am I not here?
Where would you *go* to find me,
My Beloved, My own?

What would you *do* to gain my Love,
Which is now, has ever been,
And will ever be yours,
My Beloved, My Own?

Why do you hurt me so,
As if My Love is conditioned,
On renunciation, and discipline,
On accomplishment, and merit?

Do you not Know me,
My Beloved, My Own?
Have I not shown you,
Again, and again…

I am here for you… *Always*,
Without cause, beyond conditionality,
In the Wellspring of your Heart,
Ever Present… Here…

Shining in you… As You,
And… Beyond we two,
In the Formless Ecstasy of Heaven,
My Beloved, My Own.

Be Still… and Know that I Am Love.

AN INEFFABLE "SOMETHING WONDERFUL"

When I was eleven years old or so,
I met each week with several friends,
And read passages from the Bible,
Discussing, after, the meanings.

It was not that I "knew", and taught,
But only that I was rapt in fascination,
Like the friends who gathered there,
By longing for "Something Wonderful".

At that time, I felt myself a Christian,
For the Being I imagined embodying,
That Ineffable Something Wonderful,
Was the ancient man I cherished.

But in the passing of time I discovered,
Expressed in every faith I encountered,
That Mysterious Something Wonderful,
However veiled at the hands of men.

And over time I came to see,
That it was no particular faith I loved,
But that which I imagined each embodying,
Shining as the Heart of their origin.

And over time I came to see,
That it was no particular prophet I adored,
But that which I imagined each embodying,
Shining at the Heart of their Being...

And that Something Wonderful... is Love.

STILL THE POETS STRUGGLE

What is this Beloved? A Mystery.
Love is often used to describe Her,
But the simplicity of a single word,
Is for a child's understanding.

And still the poets struggle.

Not to convey to abacus minds,
Through logic, reason, or conclusion,
But to evoke within longing Hearts,
The Fulfillment of the Soul's desire.

A Beauty beyond the judgment,
Of beautiful and ugly,
A Rapture beyond the suffering,
Of ecstatic and agonizing.

In the Garden of the Beloved

A Fullness beyond the famine,
Of satiation and hunger,
A Completion beyond the lack,
Of repose and seeking.

A Love beyond the sorrow,
Of lovable and unlovable,
A Peace beyond the endless strife,
Of repose and tumult.

But above all of these, my Friend…

The felt sense, nearer than near,
Palpable and real as your heartbeat,
Of being Loved, Held in Tender Affection,
When no form is present Loving you.

Who is, what is, this Mysterious Beloved,
Who boggles the hapless mind,
Inhabits the Intoxicated Heart,
And Fulfills the Soul's Desire?

All of these words are the Poet's breath,
Blowing softly on the flickering ember,
To ignite the Flame of Remembrance,
Of The Beloved, beyond all dualities.

Still… the poets struggle.

THE INTERIOR DESIGNER

When The Beloved took up residence in my Heart,
She cleaned house, and threw out my belongings,
Tossing hypotheses and theories of creation,
Theologies, cosmologies, and philosophies…

And any need of belief or faith.

"Wait!" I cried, I need those things, to make sense,
Of this world, of this life, of myself, and You.
But She slapped my grasping fingers, Lovingly,
And eventually… threw "me" out, as well.

And here's what cannot be explained in words,
In hypotheses, theories, or conclusions of the mind;
That I remain, as that which remained,
When at last Her housekeeping had ceased…

And the Emptiness, within, was Filled with Love.

She still Polishes, Dusts, and moves things about,
Occasionally removing, occasionally adding,
But I no longer have a say in these matters,
Surrendered, long ago, to The Interior Designer.

Miraculously, within this Emptying and Filling,
A single belief escaped the conflagration,
When all others were consumed in Her Flame,
For this Grace, I "believe", is true for us all.

In the Garden of the Beloved

WHERE LOVE ABIDES

I wander the Wilderness outside the walled villages of religion,
Not because I hold them in disdain, denying their fruitfulness,
For my Heart embraces within each, that which resonates,
And sets aside that which does not.

Nor do I deny the efficacy possible in each village,
For within the constraints of their dogmas and orthodoxies,
There have been, and will always be, those few,
Who transcend the letter of the law, Fulfilling its Spirit.

I often encounter fierce villagers standing guard at the gates,
Declaring I, a heretic, may not enter, much less embrace,
For neither do I adhere to, nor abide by their laws,
For theirs is, they say, the way and the truth.

Time and again I have pushed past these militant legalists,
And turning from the road leading to the edifice of law,
Have found my way to The Tavern of The Beloved,
Where, Intoxicated, I have reveled in Love.

Ibn Arabi so Beautifully distilled my many words:

"I profess the religion of Love.
Wherever its caravan turns along the way,
That is the belief, the faith I keep".

WHERE RIVER MEETS OCEAN

There is a place within us,
Where the river of our existence,
Meets the Ocean of our origin;
Where those waters swirl together,
And it can no longer be discerned,
Whether river has become Ocean,
Or Ocean has become river.

There is a place within us,
Where our Longing for The Beloved,
Is Fulfilled in Her Embrace,
And it can no longer be discerned,
Whether Lover has become Beloved,
Or Beloved, the Lover.

In that moment of time's dissolution,
In that place of space's vanishing,
In that ending of our existence,
We remain, as What Remains,
And our Essence is Revealed,
The Kingdom of Heaven, within,
The answer to every prayer ever uttered.

ROSE AND JASMINE

There are as many paths to God,
As there are souls on earth.

Therefore I say, "This is my experience,
Not to be confused with "Truth'".

Therefore I say, "I went this way",
Not, "This is The way".

Therefore I say, "For me, Love sufficed",
Not, "For all, Love suffices".

Therefore I say, "I know only this",
Not, "I have the answer".

Therefore I say, "These are my words",
Not, "Speak this way".

Each flower emanates a fragrance,
Unique unto its kind.

And in all my life I have never seen,
A Rose at war with Jasmine.

REAL LOVE

After The Beloved's Embrace,
Her Perfume surrounds you,
The Warmth of Her touch remains,
She makes space in your closet,
And leaves a toothbrush.

This is getting serious!

When you think you are alone,
She reminds you of Her Nearness,
With a gentle touch to the Heart,
A whispered Secret to the mind,
A tender Kiss to your Soul.

Can this really be true?!

The mind wonders in perplexity,
How such Beauty and Grace,
Can cohabit a shoddy hovel,
In which such a mess remains,
Of socks and underwear strewn.

And the Heart answers, "Real Love".

REASON'S DRUNKEN LONGING

Those of the Mind, who deride the Heart,
As delusional, moved by frivolous emotionality,
Need to spend more time with her.

And those of the Heart who dismiss the Mind,
As an arid accumulator of meaningless data,
Need to spend more time with him.

We become so easily hardened in our stance,
When we take refuge in a walled village of belief,
Behind bastions of opinion and prejudice.

I have sat and reasoned empirically with the Mind,
And can tell you he cares with fervent passion,
And is, in his own way, moved by Longing…

To Understand the Experience of the Heart.

And having drunk Wine to excess with the Heart,
I can tell you, assuredly, she is nobody's fool,
And is, in her own way, moved by reason…

To Experience what the Mind seeks to Understand.

THE PERSON, SOMEONE

I did not make myself, but found myself made,
When in birth's shock, the world appeared,
As a dream of things in space and time,
And I, a thing among them, moving.

I was not aware of myself, but became aware,
As others referred to me, and I to them,
And I, from them, came to see myself,
As a person, somebody, someone.

I lost mySelf for a time in this person, someone,
Wandering the world of form, as a thing alive,
Forgetting, in time, the Formless Radiance,
Of Existence as Aliveness Itself.

As this person, someone, I wandered so far,
From The Kingdom of Heaven, my Essence,
That I Found myself lost in forgetfulness,
In the impoverished kingdom of myself.

And I would have died there, surely, of Starvation,
Had not the Hunger of Heartbroken Longing,
Driven Heart and Mind, in desperation,
To turn their weary gaze within.

Where I found That which had never been lost,
The Spaceless, merely forgotten in space,
The Timeless, simply forgotten, in time,
My Radiant Essence forgotten…

In the person, someone.

A MOVEMENT OF LOVE AND LONGING

It was a Movement of Love and Longing,
Not a skill learned, a practice perfected,
A technique to be mastered…

This turning within, to find The Beautiful One.

It was a matter of Aching Remembrance,
Of something Known, but forgotten,
Of something Cherished beyond all things…

Then… somehow… lost.

It was a Movement of Love and Longing,
Not a posture taken, a mindset adopted,
A conclusion of the mind, arrived at…

This turning within, to find The Beloved.

Does gazing at a picture of your Love,
Remembering the Fragrance of Her Perfume,
The Intoxicating Warmth of Her Embrace...

Require discipline?

Although the mind's utility was enjoined,
And the Whole of Being engaged,
Finding Her at last, and Dying in Her arms...

Was a Movement of Love and Affection.

WAY STATIONS

There are many way stations on this Journey,
Not transient experiences had along the Way,
But enduring transmutations of Being.

We realize these arrivals only after the fact,
Wondering to ourselves in amazement,
"How and when did this happen"?

For they are not the result of understanding,
Or the product of doing this, not doing that,
But Longing, that moves both mind and heart.

Longing, in the depths of our deepest interiority,
Inextinguishable, at the Heart of our Being,
The Remembrance, of Something Known...

But forgotten.

In the Garden of the Beloved

The Warmth of Love's Light, felt faintly,
Glimmering distant, through countless veils,
Accrued over a lifetime of embodiment.

The fleeting Fragrance of Her Perfume,
Wafting teasingly on the Breeze of Grace,
Turning our spirit in search of its origin.

And Journeying to The Kingdom of Heaven,
We arrive, again and again, and again,
At the way stations of our Diminishment...

And Increase of The Beautiful One.

There is no pride of achievement in arriving,
For each station marks the impending death,
Of the self, grasping desperately after stature.

There are no enlightened ones along this Way,
Only endless Stations of Enlightening,
Where Lovers, for a time, Revel and Dance...

In ever-deepening Remembrance.

Some say the goal is to come to Perfection,
To vanish, one day, utterly and completely,
Arriving, at last, at the end of stations...

Where Lover and Beloved Dance as One.

If that is so, then She has hobbled this Fool,
For I find the Rapture of Her Presence,
In every step taken along The Way.

And the stations ahead are of no concern,
For if Her Love Shines Radiant in my Heart,
Here, imperfect as I am, still Journeying…

What need have I of Heaven?

THE GRAPEFRUIT

I sat beneath a grapefruit tree,
Mournful of my state of being.

Impatient, frustrated, despairing,
I gazed upward, tearfully.

And there, high amidst ripe fruit,
I saw the little fellow.

Yellow and ripe for the most part,
But a touch of green at the stem.

And I sighed to The Beloved,
Whispering, with a smile…

"All right. All right".

SOMEWHERE IN BETWEEN

I've fainted several times in this life,
And in that unconscious state,
Awareness of everything ceased,
Including awareness of myself.

It was, in a sense, a death.

Speaking of it after the fact,
I can say that there was nothing,
Not even myself aware of nothing,
No knowledge of nonexistence…

The very definition of unconscious.

But I have Known another Fainting,
When awareness of everything ceased,
Including awareness of myself existing,
And yet, I remained… as Existence.

Speaking of it after the fact,
I can say that there was nothing,
Not even myself aware of nothing,
And yet…

Awareness remained, aware of nothing,
Existence remained, with nothing existing,
Aliveness remained, with nothing alive,
Creativity remained, with nothing created.

The very definition of The Great Mystery.

Something Wonderful, that is not a thing,
Exists before the arising of all things,
Something Wonderful, I had dreamed of,
But could only Be in my vanishing.

I do not now dwell in that Heaven, within,
Where within and without have no meaning,
Nor do I dwell as captive to the body,
Or held hostage by the intellect…

WHERE IS THE MIND?

"Where is the mind"? asked another Heart, sitting next to me in
The Tavern of The Beloved.

"He's off at the temple of learning, seeking knowledge and
understanding". I responded, taking a sip of Wine, eyes fixed
upon the Face of The Beautiful Innkeeper.

"What knowledge will he bring, when at last he joins us"? the
Heart friend queried.

He will say, "I Am".

"And how will you respond"? asked the friend.

I will say, "I Love".

HERE IN EMBODIMENT

Although Love has long been Fulfilled,
Her Perfume Filling my besotted Heart,
Her Loving touch always upon me...

Still, my Heart bends like a desperate rose,
Here, in the dimmed Light of embodiment,
Toward the Sunlight of Her Face.

Like a lost puppy I whimper and whine,
Even as She Holds me nearer than near,
And whispers, "I'm here for you, Always".

THE UNPAID RANSOM

Since early childhood I saw the "law",
As coming from the minds of men,
Or, if coming from the voice of God,
Corrupted, after, by the minds of men.

And philosophy, likewise, held no sway,
Once I realized that its broad diversity,
Originated, too, from the minds of men,
In concepts, theories, and conjecture.

From the start it was Experience,
That captivated both heart and mind,
And abandoning reason and logic,
I took a room in the Tavern of Fools.

There, the only requirement of the law,
Was a Heart held hostage by Longing,
And a mind possessing the Wisdom,
To refuse payment of the ransom.

THE MOST BEAUTIFUL OF LUNACIES

You cannot be "converted" to Love,
It is either in your nature at birth,
Or brought to fruition over time,
By the vicissitudes of life.

Nor is Longing a "strategy" taken,
Craftily devised in logic and reason,
An affectation to be artfully acted,
In hopes of fooling The playwright.

What strange tribe this is, of Lovers,
Who, without choice in the matter,
Are broken-hearted from the start,
And broken-minded, along The Way.

Whose thoughts are ever Enraptured,
By a Mystery, ever beyond grasping,
Whose Hearts Revel and Dance,
With a Partner Unseen… by most.

Whose Longing has pierced the Veil,
And enticed The Healer of Souls,
To Abide within the Heart's Asylum,
Where our mind wanders the halls…

In the most Beautiful of Lunacies.

BEYOND HOLY AND UNHOLY

For so much of my long life,
It caused me great suffering,
That I was an unholy man;
Unrefined, dull-witted, worldly,
At times even hating God.

It became ever more clear,
That the transient moments,
Of inspiration and aspiration,
Were inconstant aberrations,
And not foundations of faith.

For time and again they left,
As quickly as they had arrived,
And I was left in bewilderment,
That inspiration had arisen at all,
In one so very far from virtue.

Yet within my weary Heart,
Longing was not extinguished,
For Love found not in scripture,
But written in wordless letters,
Upon the pages of my Soul.

And in time there came a day,
When driven, broken-hearted,
I followed that Longing within,
And found The Love of Loves,
Beyond holy and unholy…

That I Am. That we All Are.

It was myself, and yet, was not,
For "I" had vanished on The Way,
Yet remained, as The Remaining,
No longer one existing, alive,
But Alive, as Existence Itself.

And when creation and I returned,
I found, thereafter, in my Heart,
The Love I'd sought hopelessly,
Radiant amidst my imperfection,
Inherent in my Soul, and yours…

Beyond holy and unholy.

In the Garden of the Beloved

EAT!

The Pantry of my Heart is Full,
Why would I visit the marketplace,
Where the vendors of God,
Accost my spirit at every turn.

If The Beloved sent me there,
I would move among those stalls,
And do my best to find the ripe,
Among the many fruits held forth.

But these days, She bids me sit,
She, who long ago Filled my Heart,
Heaping my plate, Filling my cup,
Whispering, as if I could bear more…

"You're so skinny, my Love. Eat!"

A GUZZLER

"Show me how you drink your coffee",
The Beautiful One asked, one day,
And corrected me to sip slowly, and savor.

Departing, she blew a Kiss.

"Show me how you drink My Wine",
She asked with a sidelong glance,
And seeing that I was a Guzzler...

Embraced my Drunken Soul.

A FOOLISH PROPENSITY

Q: What or whom is this Beloved you speak of?

I don't know.

Q: How then, do you write so Lovingly of Her?

Because I Know Her Intimately.

Q: You just said you didn't know!

I said I don't know "what" or "whom".

If the Fragrance of Jasmine wafts by,
And you have no knowledge of Jasmine,
No word that names, or image that embodies,
That is the Knowing I speak of.

The Experience of Jasmine is yours,
Though "knowledge of" escapes you,
And you Feel yourself Enfolded, Embraced,
By Nameless, Formless, Sublimity.

Q: Why then, do you speak of "She"?

It's no more, I'm afraid, than a foolish propensity.

Q: How can you abide such foolishness?

When The Beautiful One possessed my Heart,
She transmuted a sober rationalist,
Into a Drunken Romantic,
Who Loves, above all…

To Love.

DANCING WITH THE BELOVED

The Art of Dancing with The Beloved,
Is in learning to let Her lead,
Till your Surrender to Diminishment,
Leaves The Beautiful One Dancing Alone.

What a Mystery, then, that not existing,
You Remain.

THE HAPPINESS OF ANOTHER

There came a day, some years ago,
When the world's suffering overcame me,
And drowning in an Ocean of Sorrow,
I wondered at a reason to continue.

Finding nothing in the world's enticements,
I sat sobbing, having lost all hope,
Until, amidst my tears, there appeared,
A vision, only of a woman's smile.

No face accompanying, but only a smile,
A smile not yet broken into laughter,
But on the brink, near bursting with joy,
Happiness, there, in the smile of another.

And in that instant, my tears transmuted,
For without thought, attention turned,
From myself, and the Ocean of sorrows,
To Happiness, there, on the face of another.

And the whole of me was Taken, wholly,
By a Happiness, Pure and Unalloyed,
A Happiness born of only one cause;
The Happiness of the Mysterious Other.

The world Vanished, and I Vanished,
And only an Unbearable Love remained,
And tears of an Unbearable Longing,
For the Happiness of the Mysterious Smiler.

When I emerged from Oblivion in Love,
And my eyes perceived, once again,
This world of countless Sorrows,
I had been Shown the reason to exist.

I Revel now, in the enjoyments of this life,
Which before, had lost their savor,
And cry, still, for the Sorrows of the world,
But constant, now, in both Joy and Sorrow,
Find Life's Greatest Happiness...

In the Happiness of another.

THE DIVINE THIEF

I cannot fathom this Mystery,
For when She draws near,
My mind falls down, Drunk...

And only my Heart remains.

How can my mind ever grasp,
How will it ever understand,
The Mystery of Her Presence...

When in Her Presence, it faints.

It cannot think, to conclude,
Or envision in imagination,
The Beauty of Her Face.

How can I hope to understand,
When The Divine Thief,
Steals my very existence...

And only Love remains.

WHERE LOVE ABIDES

I once had a Vision of God,
And asked why She appeared.

She said it was in response,
To the depth of my Longing.

I asked if there was not a Love,
Requiring no such cause.

She touched my Heart, nodding,
And smiled.

Just so, more or less veiled,
Such Love abides in each of us.

She did not speak of theology,
Or the nature of reality.

She did not reveal Her Mystery,
But in this simple gesture…

Revealed all that matters.

THE ESSENCE OF ALL THINGS

"Mercy!" cried the anguished mind,
Pleading for an end to suffering.

"Deluded friend", the Heart whispered,
"Mercy will not end your suffering".

Follow the Perfume of The Beloved,
To the Essence of All Things... within.

Where suffering and its opposite,
Mercy and its opposite are yet unborn.

And Vanishing in the arms of Grace,
Exist without Existing, yet unborn.

When the world of creation reappears,
Its infinite polarities will greet you.

But swimming now, like so many fish,
In The Essence of All Things.

THE BEAUTY OF HER FACE

A friend once asked in perplexity,
"Why do you not close your eyes,
And turning from the world of form,
Fall into the arms of The Beloved"?

"Don't blame me!" I exclaimed,
"It is She who Besotted my eyes,
So that all I behold in this world,
Is the Beauty of Her Face".

These days, when I do close my eyes,
It's nothing of my doing, but Hers,
In moments when She Whispers,
And Turning… I am no more.

BECAUSE, AFTER, IF, AND WHEN

I have been known to fall into Despair,
Believing the words of the legalists,
Who say The Beloved Loves "because"…

Loves only "after" we…
Loves only "if" we…
Loves only "when" we.

In those moments of deepest despair,
I think to put an end to this life,
And any lives that might follow thereafter.

For I would not live for even one moment,
In a life where The Beloved Loves because,
Only after… only if… only when.

But in such moments, She stays my hand,
And reveals through Love, again, and again,
The terrible deceit of the legalists.

For my imperfections have not diminished,
Nor my few virtues increased, one whit,
The Love that Fills me, through Grace.

If She will not dwell in an unclean temple,
How is it, then, that She Inhabits my Heart,
As Love, Causeless and Unconditional…

Not because, not after, not if, not when.

IN MY OLD AGE

It no longer matters what friends believe,
Or the faith they have in those beliefs,
The religion in which their heart takes refuge,
Or the philosophy that satisfies their mind.

In my old age, it's become quite simple.

However far from perfection you may be,
Are you kind-hearted and compassionate?

However cynical or bitter you've become,
Do you desire that all suffering cease?

However faint the ember of hope, within,
Do you ache for the Blessing of creation?

However weary in body, mind, and spirit,
Do you do as you're able, for Love's sake?

Yes? Then come in! I have Wine!

THE MIND IN LOVE

Good morning, Beloved, it's me again.
I've brought my bag of questions,
As I do with each morning's visit.

You know what's in there, right?
For I cannot verbalize them all,
Or articulate them, even to myself.

Somehow you read my Soul, right?
The wordless cries of Cognition,
Struggling to Know and Understand?

You do not hate me, do You, my Love,
Like those who decry my existence,
As the Hinderer of belief and faith?

For I Love you, as does the Heart,
But in a manner suited to my nature,
As You, Beautiful One, have made me.

And so, as always, I will simply sit,
And Resting in the depths Unknowing,
Feel you Flood me with Your Love.

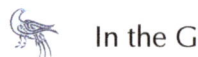 In the Garden of the Beloved

A Love that answers without answering,
The 10,000 questions in my bag,
And leaves me Wondering, as ever...

What... are... You?

HOW COULD I LEAVE YOU ON FIRE?

If, when I leave this body, I am guided,
By an Angel to the Gates of Heaven,
I will turn to gaze back, Lovingly,
At this Beautiful, Heartbroken world,
And proffering my best wishes to God,
Will loosen my hand from the Angel's,
And turning, walk again into the flames,
Bearing what water my Heart can carry...

For how could I leave you on fire?

LOVE WILL NOT FALL OUT OF ME

There've been times when I've tried to fall out of Love,
When the chaos of theologies and philosophies,
Have caused my weary mind to collapse in a heap.

For the poor fellow insisted on pouring The Mystery,
Into a template, a mold, a model of understanding,
A concise erudition of "the nature of things".

It was not enough that the Heart was Full and Radiant,
For the mind simply could not help but Wonder,
"What… is… this… Fullness… this… Radiance"?

Once, in a fit of delirium, it screamed at The Beloved,
"If you will not teach me in the language I speak,
Take your tormenting Gibberish, and go!"

But She only Brightened, Illumining his Ignorance.

Once the confounded mind, like a petulant child,
In a tantrum, hurled stones at the Gates of Heaven,
Only to have Her emerge, pinch his cheek, and whisper…

This is why I Love you.

I cannot fall out of Love, for Love will not fall out of me.
And while the mind, by nature, hungers always,
The Heart pushes away from the table…

Full and Sighing, Drunk on Love.

THIS TENDER AFFECTION

These days I find myself speaking,
In a most Tender, Loving voice,
To plants and trees, rocks and soil,
To clouds and mist, to moon and stars,
As if those things could hear my words,
And know of my Loving Affection.

In the Garden of the Beloved

I confess to concern regarding my sanity,
And the Foolish old man I've become,
Tears streaming, unprompted by thought,
Spontaneous, a flood Uncontainable,
At the drift of a cloud, or branches swaying,
Or the feel of the earth beneath my feet.

I noticed the onset of Love's Insanity,
When a beloved friend passed recently,
And the Affection in which I held them,
Being no longer watered by their presence,
Did not wither and die from that lack,
But sent roots outward, to All That Is.

Within, this Love sent roots, as well,
Beneath the shallow soil of "who" I am,
To the deepest Interiority of "what" I am,
And Blossomed there, at the Heart of Being,
As an Affection, near Unbearable,
For the simple fact of existing.

Thankfully, no one has witnessed me,
Whispering Thankfulness to a fallen leaf,
Or I would surely be locked away,
And, gazing out an asylum window,
Would tear up at the incredible Beauty,
Of paint peeling on the window sill,
And the Quality of evening Light…

Upon All that Is.

DELIGHT

He handed me a glass of water,
All there is, is Consciousness,
Flavorless, without quality or attribute".

Mind said, "Fascinating. Let's consider this",
Heart said, "Flavorless? Why should I care"?

I handed him a Cup of Wine,
And said, "All there is, is Love, my friend,
Our existence, the Union of Water and Grape.

And in this most Rapturous Romance,
Of Nonexistent Existence, and existence,
Lovers Dance in Delight.

SHOULD AND SHOULD NOT

When I do what I've been told I "should",
In relationship with The Beautiful One,
Time and again, She abandons my Heart.

Yet, whatever I do, if I am *Moved* to do,
By the BitterSweet Ache of Love and Longing,
Even if that doing is what I "should not"…

She Embraces my Soul, and I Swoon.

In this Way I am Taught, in every moment,
By the Brightness or dimming of Her Light,
By the ebb and Flow of Her Radiance...

What I "should" and "should not".

IN THE NATURE OF THINGS

Asking the mind not to ask anymore,
Is like asking a bird not to sing or fly,
For it's simply in its nature to do so.

Long ago The Beloved inhabited my Heart,
Yet with every breath the mind still asks,
"What is this? What's going on, here"?

It is in Her nature to be Incomprehensible,
In the mind's to seek comprehension,
And in the Heart's to Revel in Experience.

In the Sky of The Beloved's Vastness,
The mind continues its songful flight,
As is its nature.

In The Tavern of The Beloved,
The Heart continues its Drunken Dance,
As is its nature.

And The Beautiful One Embraces each,
According to their nature.

THE NEED FROM WHICH THESE THINGS ARISE

As a child, I sought Her in religion,
By many names, in many forms.

Growing older, I sought for Her,
In philosophies, vast and varied.

And older still, I looked at last,
Into reason, logic, and empiricism.

But when She Possessed my Heart,
She did not tell me Her name.

And yet… I love Her every name.

She did not speak of philosophies,
Or utter a word regarding "truth".

And yet… I understand our need.

Nor did she explain, through reason,
The nature of "reality".

And yet… I understand our quest.

The Beloved, Possessing my Heart,
Has never spoken of these things.

And yet… She taught me to Understand,
And in Compassion, to Respect…

The need from which these things arise.

THE BELOVED'S CUP

I followed the Path of Knowledge,
The mind seeking the Source of "I Am",
And found, to my enduring astonishment,
That the search for Knowledge, led to Love.

Now, I follow the Path of Love,
Drunk, at The Tavern of The Beloved,
And find, to my enduring astonishment,
That Love's Ignorance, leads to Knowledge.

The Water of Knowledge, the Grape of Love,
Are now, to my enduring astonishment,
No longer two, in The Wine sipped from…
The Beloved's Cup.

THE DANCE OF HEART AND MIND

Is it You, Beloved, or my own Soul,
That Fills the Heart of my Being,
With Love, Causeless and Eternal,
This Ecstasy without opposite?

When I Remember Your Face,
I, and the manifest world Vanish.
Falling into the depths of my Soul,
I, and the manifest world Vanish.

Could it be my Soul is that juncture,
Where You and I are Not Two,
Where river meets Ocean,
And those Waters are Not Two?

The Mind, in Wonder, seeks to know,
While The Heart Sighs in Surrender.
They Dance, together, as Rumi said,
In Astounded, Lucid Confusion.

THIS EXQUISITE UNALONENESS

I do not write to declare or assert,
To instruct or inform as if I "know",
To hold forth my Experience as "truth",
Or describe the nature of "reality".

Any assertion, seemingly emphatic,
Is but a question cloaked in certitude;
"Friend, have you Known, do you Feel,
This Radiance at the Heart of Being"?

In the Garden of the Beloved

For paradoxical though it may seem,
While The Beloved Fills my Heart,
With a Fullness, Vanquishing need,
I long for the company of Drunkards...

In this Most Exquisite Unaloneness.

HEARTBREAKINGLY BEAUTIFUL

If the world, without, and "self", within,
Had not broken my Heart so deeply,
I would not have sought my Essence,
In the Ecstasy of Nonexistent Existence.

But returning from Unmanifest Heaven,
To the Dream of manifest creation,
I no longer lamented the world, without,
But found its play of joy and sorrow to be...

Heartbreakingly Beautiful.

And returning from Unmanifest Heaven,
To the Dream of a manifest self,
I no longer bemoaned that fellow, within,
But found him, in all his imperfection, to be...

Heartbreakingly Beautiful.

For the Love that I Am, when "I" am not,
Imbues me now, in the Dream of "I" am,
And existence, beyond the gates of Eden,
While Heartbreaking, is, in the same breath…

Exquisitely Beautiful.

IT SEEMS

It seems not to be a matter of belief,
For The Beautiful One, it seems,
Cared little for what I thought of Her

Nor was it, it seems, a matter of faith,
For having clung to it for a time,
That ember had long since dimmed.

Rather, it seems, that bereft of these,
'Twas Desperate Love and Longing,
That turned The Beloved's Gaze.

For Love, it seems… draws Love.

WHY BREATHE HER PERFUME?

Why breathe the Perfume of The Beloved,
Why sip from the Cup of Her Wine,
Why fall into the Warmth of Her Embrace,
Where no one seen, Embraces?

Because in that breathing, sipping, falling,
The breather, sipper, faller Vanishes,
And what remains in that Sweet Oblivion,
Is the Fulfillment of the Heart's Desire…

The Ecstasy of Existence, before existing.

BLISS

There are those who forsake Bliss,
As ephemeral and transient,
A phenomenon to be dismissed,
Binding us ever more deceptively,
To the experiencer self.

They do not Know of that Ecstasy,
Which arises only in the Vanishing,
Of all Ecstasy and Agony…

And their experiencer.

"A dangerous sweet", they say,
Not to be confused with "Truth",
Not to be mistaken, tragically,
For the Absolute, without Qualities,
For the Absolute, without Attributes.

They do not Know of that Ecstasy,
Which arises only in the Vanishing,
Of all qualities and attributes.

This Bliss cannot bind you to the self,
For no self remains in its Dissolution.
Nor can you dismiss this Ecstasy,
For "you" no longer exist to do so.
Bliss is the Nature, Pure and Unalloyed…

Of Nonexistent Existence.

GRACE

Grace does not hold an abacus in one hand,
Tallying worthiness and merit,
Or a Rubik's cube in the other,
Challenging us to "Figure it out".

Grace knows nothing of such cruelties.

Grace is the power that comes alive
When Attention, wandering without,
Turns within, Journeying inward,
In quest of The Heart's Desire.

Divine Remembrance… a movement of Grace.

From the first awakening of Longing,
To the first turning within,
Through the long, inward trek,
And our vanishing into Pure Being…

Every step… a movement of Grace.

In the Garden of the Beloved

Grace is the power of "Fruitioning",
Of Seed to Blossom,
Of Ember to Flame,
Of Longing to Fulfillment.

The Seasons of Love... a movement of Grace.

Grace is the gravity of Formless Pure Being,
Pulling our sense of separate existence,
To its Ultimate Oblivion...
And Unimaginable Benediction.

The Beloved's tug on our Heart... a movement of Grace.

The Heart's Unbearable Longing,
And its Absolute Fulfillment,
The mind's Endless Wonder,
And its Surrender to Unknowing.

Longing and Wonder... movements of Grace.

Grace is not a "consequence",
Of worthiness or merit,
Of conditionality,
Of causality.

Causeless Love... a movement of Grace.

Do we choose to have a Heart
Drunk with Longing?
Do we choose to have a mind
Held captive by Wonder?

Surrender… a movement of Grace.

It is Grace that calls us,
Grace that moves us,
And Grace that sustains us,
Until we Vanish…

In its welcoming arms.

GRACE IS…

Grace is the Ocean flowing into the river,
Not the other way 'round.

Grace is The Destination Arriving at you,
When you have not yet arrived.

Grace is an impossible Blossoming,
While you are yet still a bud.

Grace is being Discovered,
By that which you sought to discover.

Grace is being Embraced,
By that which you sought to embrace.

Grace is being Possessed by Perfection,
While you are yet far from Perfect.

Grace is Love, drawn to Itself, Here…
In the Heart of your Deepest Interiority.

NEARER THAN NEAR

I never called my mother, "Mother",
That was far too formal, too distant,
For the Beautiful being I called "Mom",
Who held me Nearer than near.

Nor did I call my father, "Father",
That being far too formal, too distant,
For the Beautiful being I called "Dad",
Who held me Dearer than dear.

Nor have I ever called You "Lord",
For that is far too formal, too distant,
For the Tender, Loving Intimacy,
With which You Enfold my Soul...

Nearer than near.

AGAIN, AGAIN, AND AGAIN

So many of the furnishings,
And decorative items in my home,
Are tattered, worn, and threadbare,
Like their life-worn owner.

Many things here were once broken,
But rather than being discarded,
Have been mended, Lovingly,
By their broken owner.

For the Owner of my Soul,
The Beautiful One, The Mystery,
Has mended, again, again, and again,
This threadbare, broken Heart…

And Filled it with Love.

LOVE'S UNIMAGINABLE GRACE

I thought She would make me perfect,
I thought She would make me wise,
I thought She would end my suffering,
And I would be continuously happy.

But all She did was Fill my weary Heart,
With Fullness, Completion, and Bliss,
And the Ever-Present Radiance,
Of a Love without cause or condition.

She did not make me Perfect,
But the Wonder of Unimaginable Grace,
Is that Her Radiant Perfection Shines,
In the Heart of this imperfect vessel.

She did not make me Wise,
But the Wonder of Unimaginable Grace,
Is that Her Radiant Wisdom Imbues,
A mind bound in ignorance and knowledge.

She did not end my suffering,
But the Wonder of Unimaginable Grace,
Is that an Ecstasy without opposite,
Accompanies even my deepest sorrow.

If I were a Perfect man, full of Wisdom,
My lesser self, alchemized into Gold,
Who, then, would Wonder at Her Presence,
In such a virtuous, sanctified temple.

But The Beloved's Presence in this hovel,
Imperfect, Foolish, and home to sorrows,
Is a Wonder beyond all reckoning,
And proof to those having lost all hope…

Of Love's Unimaginable Grace.

DRINK!

Without Heart, the mind is barren,
And without Flower, lacks Fragrance,
Without Fragrance, lacks Fruit,
Without Fruit, does not nourish.

The mind "knows" of Fruit,
In words, concepts, and images,
But the heart Savors the Fragrance,
And Tastes the Flavor of Love.

The vintage is not the Flavor,
The grapes are not the Wine,
The Wine is not the Tasting,
Knowledge "of" is not Experience.

Drink!

IF YOU'RE LUCKY

Some speak of the unprovable,
And ask you to have faith.

Others hold forth their "beliefs",
As if they were facts.

Some break out a whiteboard,
Asserting, "All is Consciousness".

If you're lucky, you'll meet a poet,
Who makes no sense at all.

Luckier still, you'll meet one,
Who, without speaking a word…

Ignites the Ember in your Heart.

THE UNSEEN HAND OF LOVE

How did The Beloved seek me?
By moving me to seek Her.

By burning the house of my self,
So that I might flee.

By sending me into the Desert,
So that I might be free of walls.

By filling my mind with Wonder,
So that I might ask.

By filling my Heart with Longing,
So that I might cry out.

By removing all hope of victory,
So that I might, at last, Surrender.

In countless ways, the movement,
Of the unseen hand of Love.

WITH WHOM... I DO NOT KNOW

However saddened I may become,
At the suffering inherent in this life,
The joy, inherent, is there, as well,
For both exist At Once in this Madness,
Known to those who Love.

And Something Else is there, as well,
Whether we sob, collapsed in sorrow,
Or laugh, dancing in the arms of joy,
Something that is back, behind, before,
The dualities of joy and sorrow.

Something untouched and unmoved,
By the ever-vacillating experience,
Of polarities, and all that lies between,
Something that does not end them,
But strangely, Accompanies them.

It is an Ecstasy, if I must use a word,
But an Ecstasy without opposite,
That Shines at the Heart of Being,
Even as within the peripheral sky,
Opposites come, go, ebb, and flow.

What is this Rapturous Radiance?
Is it the Soul, as some would assert,
Or the Presence of God, within us,
Or any number of things declared,
By the many faiths as "Truth"?

I write of "She", "The Beautiful One",
But know that those are only the words,
Of a Foolish old man, struggling to say,
As Attar said much better , long ago,
"I am in Love, but with Whom…

I do not know".

NAME AND FORM

Don't call Me "The Beloved", She said.
Don't call Me "The Beautiful One".
Don't call Me anything at all.

Don't imagine Me Transcendent, She said.
Don't imagine Me as Immanent.
Don't imagine Me at all.

Let your Attention Fall, Heartlong,
Into the depths of your Deepest Interiority.
Vanish, into the Essence of What You Are.

Don't call it Soul, She said.
Don't call it Atman.
Don't call it anything at all.

Don't imagine it as spirit, She said.
Don't imagine a formless "something".
Don't imagine it at all.

Vanish there, along with all of creation,
And, no longer existing as one existent,
Exist in the Ecstasy of Nonexistence.

When you return from that Heaven,
Give Me a name, if you must.
Imagine Me, if you must.

But do not insist that others name Me so,
Or imagine Me in the way you have,
For neither of these are What I Am.

Remember, above all else remembered,
I am no word spoken or image imagined,
But Am, above all else, Love.

Forgetting this…
You have remembered nothing,
And have forgotten everything.

MAYBE WE CAN

A tiny bird flew across my path today,
And, compassion filling my Heart,
I wished, with all of my Heart,
That I could Bless that little Being.

And in that instant I realized,
That I held the same Loving wish,
For all that my eyes beheld,
Both sentient and insentient.

If only I could satisfy this desire,
That fills my eyes with tears,
To Bless every atom of Creation,
With The Beloved's Benediction.

In the Garden of the Beloved

Is there a Power, I wondered,
In this Radiant Presence, within,
That transcends the binding laws,
Holding sway in manifestation?

Can I, can we, through Love, Enliven,
And Illumine with Grace, the world,
In ways that transcend and confound,
The dominion of the known?

Maybe I can; maybe we can.

WATER TO WINE

Most live their lives,
As an upstream river,
Far from the Ocean,
Into which, one day,
They will pour.

There is no savor,
In the water of their life,
No remembrance of,
Or taste of the Ocean,
To which they flow.

Living life from the Soul,
We Abide not upstream,
But at that juncture,
Where river meets Ocean,
And those waters, merging…

Are turned to Wine.

HELD

Farud ud-Din Attar, the Sufi poet,
Was unquestionably a Friend,
Held Dear by The Beautiful One.

Yet he did not flee the Mongols,
And fell cruelly, there in Nishapur,
To a warrior's bloodied sword.

Friendship with The Beloved,
Does not spare us worldly harm,
Or ensure life to those we love.

Rather, it Enraptures our Heart,
And Illumines our Deepest Interiority,
With a Light, inextinguishable.

A Love that Envelopes our Being,
Even as the body falls to the sword,
Or succumbs to wretched disease.

Not a conceptual abstraction,
Or a matter of "belief" or "faith",
But palpable, visceral, real.

The Ecstasy of Nonexistent Existence,
Alive, in the Heart of our Being,
As the Heart of our Being.

And whatever befalls us in this life,
Occurs surrounded in that Light,
And we are Accompanied, Embraced…

Held.

LET ME DANCE

What do I care for a Transcendent Absolute,
Devoid of qualities and attributes?!

Give me the Rapturous Ecstasy,
Of The Beloved's Embrace!

Let me Dance with The Beautiful One,
While I exist to Dance.

For if, in Heaven, She and I are no more,
I will linger here, in sha' Allah*.

Let me gaze upon Her Beautiful Face,
As all that fills my sight.

For if, in Heaven, The Beloved is hidden,
I will linger here, in sha' Allah.

Let me hear Her wordless Whisper,
In still silence, and clamorous din.

For if, in Heaven, Her Voice is unheard,
I will linger here, in sha' Allah.

Let me savor the taste of Her Radiance,
As the Wine of my own Existence.

For if, in Heaven, The Tavern is closed,
I will linger here, in sha' Allah.

Let me feel Her Touch, palpable and real,
As a Sublime Radiance, within.

For if, in Heaven, She is far removed,
I will linger here, in sha' Allah.

Let me inhale Her Fragrance,
As the Perfume of Grace, here on Earth.

For if, in Heaven, Love is unscented,
I will linger here, in sha' Allah.

What do I care for a Transcendent Absolute,
Devoid of qualities and attributes?!

In the Garden of the Beloved

Give me the Rapturous Ecstasy,
Of The Beloved's Embrace!

* God willing.

ONE THING

On this Path of Love and Surrender,
It does not matter how you sit or breathe,
How you hold your hands thus, or thus,
Whether you remain still, or move about,
Whether your eyes are closed, or open,
Whether thoughts are silenced, or chatter on.

On this Path of Love and Surrender,
It matters naught what you believe in,
The description of "reality" to which you hold,
Which faith you pour your Longing into,
The dogma you declare fiercely as "truth",
Or the prophet to whom your Heart is drawn.

I'm betting you can guess, my friend,
The single thing that matters upon this Way,
The one thing which, when lacking, within,
Makes of techniques, mere fruitless gestures,
Makes stillness and movement, irrelevancies,
Makes of belief and faith, a withered rose.

I'm betting you can guess, my friend,
The One Thing which, Radiant in your Heart,
Illumines the Way for the enquiring mind,
Nourishes whichever technique you employ,
Moves with you, even in the din of the world,
And Guides your weary Heart, Homeward.

GREATNESS

The Greatness of a teacher,
Or any being, for that matter,
Is not in their shakti,
Or powers of any kind.

Not in eloquence,
In intellect,
Or charisma,
Or the numbers of their following.

Not in "credentials",
Or stature of any kind.

The Greatness of a teacher,
Or any being, for that matter,
Is the extent to which the vessel
Has been subsumed by Love.

WHERE DO I BEGIN AND END?

In spiritual childhood I was taught,
You are not this body,
Not this chattering mind,
Not the individuated person,
You feel yourself to be.

These were well-intended lies,
Partialities presented as "truth",
Mere pedagogical means,
To break the chains of bondage,
To body, mind, and person.

But when the salt doll of my self,
Drowned, Dissolving in the Ocean,
Of Nonexistent Existence,
I returned to the shore as Salt Water,
And declared to the sands of time:

I Am Transcendent and Immanent,
I Am The Ocean, and the Wave,
I Am The Sky, and the Cloud,
I am unmanifest, and manifest.

Tell me, if you can…
Where do I begin and end?

I WOULD NOT VEIL HER SO

Question:
What is it that disengages,
From all that appears in Awareness,
To Rest in and as Awareness?

Answer:
It is the focal point of Awareness,
Attention, that moves here and there,
In fascination with this and that.

Question:
What is it, then, that moves Attention,
From its diverse fascinations,
To Rest, unmoving, in its Source?

Answer:
It is The Beloved that moves Attention,
From its diverse fascinations,
To Rest, unmoving, within Herself.

Question:
Ah! So The Friend is Awareness itself,
Within which all appears,
Dances for a time, then vanishes?

Answer:
I would not Veil Her so.

ONLY LOVERS KNOW

If The Beloved abides within my Heart,
How is it I am Filled with Longing?

Why do I act as one Famished,
When She has laid a Feast within me?

How can I Thirst, when I am Drowning,
In the Ocean of Her Love?

What is this ache for Her Embrace,
When She holds me so close, I Vanish?

Are these tears of Joy or Sorrow, here,
In the eyes of my Soul, Enraptured?

Only Lovers know.

THE DANCE OF JOY AND SORROW

Joy and Sorrow dance together, here,
One never letting go of the others hands,
While the Divine Musician stands apart,
Allowing each their place upon the floor.

Sorrow is not denied its mournful turning,
Nor Joy alone allowed its whirling delight,
For these two dancing together, as one,
Lead us to the Ecstasy beyond dualities.

For a time I danced alone with Joy and Sorrow,
Then turned, to Sway in The Beloved's arms,
Taking up, thereafter, the Instrument of my Soul,
To Return to the floor, Playing while Dancing…

Laughing and Crying once more…

But accompanied, now, by Ecstasy.

WHEN THE PAINTER SIGHS "BE"

Upon the canvas of Awareness,
The senses paint the picture of life,
In perceptions and sensations,
Which mind then varnishes in knowing.

The gist of this affair, as I see it,
Is not to live transcendent as canvas,
Or lose one's self in paint and varnish,
But to live where paint meets canvas.

In the Ecstasy of Existence's Birth,
Where canvas, paint, and varnish,
As mere ideas in the mind of God,
First move from formlessness to form.

There, where we Are, but not yet are,
Where "Am" exists before "I",
Where Song exists before sound,
Dance as Delight, not yet a dancer.

For you are there, before "you" are,
In that Water before the river of you,
In that Sky before the cloud you seem,
In that Timeless, Spaceless Instant…

When The Painter sighs, "Be".

THE JOURNEY

From Eden to the womb,
From the womb to this world,
Within this world, our Journey,
Of Return.

From Nonexistent Existence,
To Existence as a thing existing,
And in that form, the Journey,
Of Return.

Neither a thing existent,
Nor Nonexistent, Am I,
For The Beloved Possesses me,
In the Madness of Both…

On the Journey of Return.

SIMPLY BECAUSE I AM

I reveled in the praise of my teachers,
And saw how in receiving good grades,
Mom and Dad were happy and proud.

And so, I sought academic stature,
That I might gain praise, or so I thought,
But truly, it was only Love I sought.

I saw how the girl I found beautiful,
Was drawn to certain qualities,
And features of a certain kind.

And so, I sought romantic stature,
That I might be adored, or so I thought,
But truly, it was only Love I sought.

I saw how those in my profession,
Admired and respected their peers,
With knowledge, skill, and experience.

And so, I sought professional stature,
That I might gain respect, or so I thought,
But truly, it was only Love I sought.

In every aspect of life I came to rely,
On the estimation of myself, by others,
For the sense of my own self "worth".

 In the Garden of the Beloved

Worth as one praised,
Worth as one desired,
Worth as one respected…

Worth as one Lovable.

Somewhere along the way, I lost,
The Fullness, Completion, and Bliss,
Inherent in my Essence, Shining…

Simply because I Am.

Somewhere along the way, I lost,
The Experience at the Heart of Being,
Of Love Shining, without condition…

Simply because I Am.

What irony that the pain of bondage,
To the intercessor self, bound in stature,
Was the very fire that drove me…

Within, to my Essence, long forgotten.

Where, Held in The Beloved's Embrace,
Conditionality burned in the Fire of Love,
I Swoon in the Ecstasy of Being…

Simply because I Am.

IT OCCURRED TO ME

It occurred to me…

There was a time when my Soul Shone, unobscured,
By all that would accrue upon my Naked Innocence,
When the Ecstasy of Being was unalloyed by selfhood,
And I existed as my Essence.

There was a time, before I learned a language,
Before the inner voice began its endless dialog,
And I came to feel my self as the thinker,
When I was simply Perception.

There was a time before all that is experienced,
Was wrapped in words, concepts, and images,
Overlaying every perception with the already known,
A time when I was simply Immediacy.

There was a time, before the felt sense of my self,
Qualified and conditioned in countless ways,
Came to feel dense, isolated, and alone,
A time when I was simply Experience.

There was a time, before boy-girl; fat-thin, gifted-dim;
Smart-dull; attractive-unattractive; admired-disdained,
A time before qualifications and attributions,
When I simply Was.

And I wondered if, before these Veils enshrouded me,
The Ecstasy of Being I sought so desperately,
Might simply be the Nature of what I Am, Before.

And so I Journeyed within, back, behind, before,
All that had accrued upon my naked Innocence,
Until only Perception Remained.

Past the felt sense of myself as a person,
Qualified and judged by myself and others,
Until only Experience Remained.

Past the attributes that had defined the person,
Birthing a relentless concern for stature,
In the eyes of others, and in my own.

Past the words, concepts, and images that cloaked,
And dulled every perception with the already known,
Until only Immediacy Remained.

Within, past all that was not my Essence I Journeyed,
Until I, and all that existed, Vanished utterly,
And somehow, impossibly…

I Remained, not as "I", but Existence Itself.

And Returning, I saw that it had been as I'd thought,
For the Ecstasy of Being is simply the Nature,
Of what we Are, before we are.

WONDER

Some see the butterflies birth,
As the fruition of a question,
A metamorphosis of the unknown,
Into the known, birthing wisdom.

I see the butterflies birth,
As the fruition of an answer,
A metamorphosis of the known,
Into the unknown, birthing Wonder.

For in the birthing of every answer,
A thousand questions are cocooned,
And Wisdom, gained not from knowledge,
But by Reveling in the Infinite Unknown.

REMEMBRANCE

In Remembrance, we are not asleep,
And yet, we abandon the world,
And our many cares within it.

In Remembrance, we are not dead,
And yet, we abandon our life, our self,
Surrendering to Exquisite Oblivion.

In Remembrance, is a forgetting,
Of all but The Beloved's Face,
In which world and self are no more.

Be of good cheer, do not despair,
This Vanishing of the world, created,
And your self, created, a part of it.

For in the end of all things is revealed,
What imagination cannot conceive,
That no longer existing, you Remain…

In the Heaven of Nonexistent Existence,
The Fulfillment of the Heart's Desire,
The Answer to every prayer uttered…

The rememberer, Forgotten.

I AM NOT, YET AM

I Dance with Her daily,
In the Dance of, "Here I Am",
In the Dance of, "I Am You".

This is the Great Confoundment.

Twirling in time, I Swoon,
And time is forgotten,
Yet… I Am.

This is the meaning of Eternal.

Spinning in space, I Vanish,
And all "things" with me,
Yet... I Remain.

This is the meaning of Infinite.

Here, I see Her, there,
But in Her Embrace...
Oh! I am Not, yet Am!

This is the meaning of Love.

YES, AND YES

I am not "meditating", but Remembering.
Not in thought or image of something known,
Outside myself, something "other", there,
But a Feeling of my Essence, my Soul, Here.

And in that Instant of Remembrance,
Before words, thoughts, or images can arise,
The Whole of my Being Sighs in Ecstasy,
As the rememberer Vanishes in Her Presence.

"In Her Presence"? they asked,
"Was it not your own Essence, your Soul,
That you held as the object of Remembrance,
Not something 'other', outside, there"?

Yes, and Yes.

WHY WOULD I CLOSE MY EYES?

But... I don't want to close my eyes,
I told The Beautiful One, The Beloved,
And make that Journey so deep within,
To Heaven, at the Heart of Being.

The only reason I once closed them,
Was to find You, and Die in Your arms.
And I did find You... and I did Die There,
In the Ecstasy of nonexistent Existence.

But... when Creation appeared once again,
And I a part of it, I found You... Here,
A Divine Stowaway, inhabiting my Heart,
Within me... in Creation... Everywhere.

Why, now, would I close these sated eyes,
And shut out Your Manifest Beauty,
To seek You, within, as Unmanifest Love,
When now... there is nowhere Love is not.

I only close them now, when I cannot resist,
Your Perfume, and the pull of Your Embrace,
Calling home my Wandering Attention,
From its Enjoyment of You as this world.

You have made Creation, not a veil,
But the shawl in which You are wrapped,
This body, not an imprisoning cage,
But the foreclosure You have Inhabited...

And furnished with Love.

UNKNOWING

My mind has lost its will,
To seek knowledge and understanding.
It no longer dreams of resolution,
To a Mystery beyond comprehension.

For after impassioned consideration,
It has concluded, rationally, empirically,
That Unknowing IS the resolution,
Any sane person will come to.

And from this Pregnant Fact is birthed...
The mind's Surrender,
The Heart having long ago Drowned,
In Love.

HERE AND THERE

There is a... a Space, Within,
A Place at the Very Heart of our Being,
Where Nothing exists, but Existence.

Not a space, of course, or a place, really,
But although unseen, ungraspable, "There",
It is Palpable, Visceral, Experienced "Here".

The Kingdom of Heaven, our Inner Sanctum,
"There", yet closer than the jugular, "Here",
The Essence we Are, before "we" are...

The "Am", before "I Am".

I will not speak for you, or others,
And become, thus, yet another theologian,
Preaching the "Truth" of all things.

But perhaps you have tasted this Wine,
Even if only as the Softest Ambience,
That Imbues, Surrounds, Enfolds in Love?

I am not in accordance with those,
Who pronounce this Essence as transcendent,
Beyond all qualities and attributes.

For when "I" Died, yet Remained,
An Attribute like none other was Revealed,
"There", at the End of all things...

Where Beginning and End do not exist.

A Rapture, an Ecstasy, beyond expression,
Beyond all dualities, without opposite,
"There", in the Heaven of Nonexistent Existence...

Where Heaven and Hell do not exist.

And a touch of that Ecstasy followed me "Here",
When "I" and Creation returned from "There",
So that "I" was never quite "myself" again…

Where self in form and formless Soul coexist.

Existing "Here" as myself, but… not,
Moving in space and time, but… not,
Being both "Here" and "There"…

Where Space, Time do not exist.

Wounded and broken in my Humanity,
But accompanied, through that Imperfection,
By that Rapturous Perfection, Shining…

Where Perfect and Imperfect do not exist.

IN THE GARDEN OF TIME

"What have I done wrong"?
The ripening fruit bemoaned,
While, burgeoning with nectar,
And rich with the colors of fruition,
A little green remained near the stem.

In the Garden of the Beloved

"Surely, this is my fault!"
The tender bud lamented,
When, upon first opening to sunlight,
The promise of flowering revealed,
Its delicate petals remained yet veiled.

Some of our deepest wounds,
Are judgements, self-inflicted,
Endless paper cuts upon our spirit,
Made by an inherently imperfect "self",
Despising its imperfection.

When in fact, the green-stemmed fruit,
The infant petals in a sheltering bud,
Are as they should be, in their time,
On schedule to arrive, in their time,
In this Dream of passing seasons.

For here, in The Garden of Time,
What is not yet, becomes what is,
And what is, becomes what was,
And our manifest Being, ever ripening,
Is not yet, now, as it will be, then.

On this Path of Love and Surrender,
Tend gently the seedling of your Heart,
Doing the needful, as you are able,
Then Surrendering, giving yourself over,
Sweet unripened...

To The Beloved Gardener.

A MADMAN

"Are those tears of joy or sorrow"? they asked.

A Madman has no answer, I replied,
For the Transcendent Beloved,
Is Immanent in my Heart as Love,
Making a mess of discernment,
And my Soul, although Radiant beyond duality,
Still sobs at the fall of a sparrow.

WHEN THE PAVEMENT ENDS

Early on Intellect leads the way,
As the cart of Love, laden with Longing,
Begins its Journey to the Kingdom of Heaven,
On the well paved roads of belief and faith.

For the Intellect is the master of the map,
Conversant in words, symbols, and directions,
Able to decipher from these, where to go,
And where to refrain from going.

The roads of religion are well tended,
Lest you be jostled, and lose your faith,
And if reason and doubt arise along the way,
Inns abound to comfort and refresh.

But when the paved way ends in dirt road,
And dirt road vanishes into rock strewn path,
And rock strewn path into trackless Wilderness,
The Intellect, at a loss, stares blankly ahead.

There, where the known vanishes into Wonder,
The Heart takes up the reins of longing,
And burning the maps of dogma for warmth,
Brings forth from its cloak, the Flask of Love.

For only a Drunken Heart can Feel the Way,
From the mind's conclusion of what we are not,
To the Rapturous Experience of what we Are,
In the Ecstasy of Nonexistent Existence.

FULFILLMENT

When they cry, "Come, eat!"
I cannot rouse myself and trudge,
To the table of belief and faith,
For the Feast of Love is Here,
At the Inn of Satisfaction.

When they cry, "Come, drink!"
I cannot lift myself and stumble,
To the well of religion and theology,
For I am far too Drunk to walk,
Here, at the Tavern of The Beloved.

When they cry, "Come, look!"
I cannot turn these sated eyes,
To read endless "proofs" of "Truth",
For the Beautiful Face that I behold,
Is more Real than any word.

When they cry, "Come, purchase!"
I cannot budge my Empty cart,
For the Fullness that it bears,
Leaves no room for the "acquired",
Wheels broken by the weight of Love.

THE CONFLUENCE

I no longer ache for Heaven,
I no longer pine for Union,
I no longer aspire to Paradise,
Or the Vanishing of self and Creation,
In Existence as That which remains.

For when I and Creation reappeared,
From Union's Nonexistent Existence,
The river of Longing, flowing that way,
Was met by a River of Love, flowing this way,
And in that Confluence, I Live, Swirling.

Awash in the Fulfillment of All Longing,
Even as Longing continues to arise,
But welling up, now, from within its Fulfillment,
In a Maelstrom circle of both at once,
Here, at the Confluence of Longing and Love.

Here, the Veil of manifestation remains,
But no longer obscuring Her Beautiful Face,
No longer hiding from the Yearning Soul,
The Fulfillment of its Heart's Desire,
The answer to every Prayer ever uttered.

It is no wonder they call this Madness,
For I cry, now, more than ever before,
But cannot discern the nature of the tears,
Whether they are born of separation's sorrow,
Or the Rapture of The Beloved's Embrace.

How can I Long for the Ecstasy of Heaven,
When She is Here, in the beating of my Heart,
Walking within me, in the Garden of Creation,
Heaven being simply "more" of This, Here, Now,
And all desire for "more" having Vanished...

Here, in the Confluence of Longing and Fulfillment.

SILENCE, STILLNESS, PEACE

My home is very near a busy road,
But Sitting in its lush garden,
The din and clamor, so close by,
While deemed by some, disruptive,
Is to me a Reminder that Silence,
Has naught to do with sound.

For hearing the myriad notes of Life,
Whether melodious or dissonant,
Within, my Soul's attention is elsewhere,
Intoxicated at The Tavern of The Beloved,
Where Enraptured, it cups its ears and asks,
"Hmm, did you say something"?

My mind moves in continuous thought,
But Resting within myself,
The flow of words and images,
While deemed by some, a distraction,
Is to me a Reminder that Stillness,
Has naught to do with movement.

For as thoughts and images flow,
Whether pleasurable or discordant,
Within, my Soul's attention is elsewhere,
Entranced by the Face of The Beloved,
Where, without turning from Her,
It gestures, "You go on ahead".

The psyche's weather roils, ever changing,
But Abiding as the formless Sky,
The inconstancy of calm and catastrophe,
While deemed by some, a hindrance,
Is to me a Reminder that Peace,
Has naught to do with change.

In the Garden of the Beloved

For whether the vicissitudes of emotion,
Bring sunlit joy or darkening sorrow,
Within, my Soul's attention is elsewhere,
Lost in Reverie of The Changeless One,
Ever Radiant in the Heart of Being,
Timeless, Spaceless, Objectless.

Abandoning silence and clamor,
We become Silence.

Abandoning stillness and motion,
We become Stillness.

Abandoning peace and unrest,
We become Peace.

Abandoning all dualities,
We become our Essence.

THE GREAT MYSTERY

"Around one question," my life orbits,
It's gravity pulls me against life's inertia,
Always near, however far I wander,
For the mundane questions of my daily life,
Only Dance like melodies upon this Chord…

"What is this, to be Alive"?

My Soul spoke it when I emerged,
From the womb's darkness and warmth,
Into the cold light of manifest existence,
And I shuddered in shock and awe,
As space, time, and objects appeared…

What happened?
Where am I?
What is this?
What is this feeling,
Of existing as "something"?

There was no time… and then there was.
There was no space… and then there was.
I existed, unaware of myself and other,
But then, suddenly, found "myself" a thing alive,
An object, among countless others…

What happened?
Where am I?
What is this?
What is this feeling,
Of existing in a Dream of dualities?

Whence I began, I do not remember,
When This will end, I cannot foresee,
What I am, is beyond my mind's grasp,
As I am carried along, overwhelmed,
In the River of manifest experience.

What happened?
Where am I?
What is this?
What is this feeling,
Of Fathomless Mystery?

Most who give thought to The Question,
Accept what they are told by others,
Building walls of "knowledge" and "belief",
Taking refuge in articles of faith, unprovable,
To keep The Wilderness of Unknowing at bay…

What happened?
Where am I?
What is this?
What is this feeling,
Of existing, isolated and alone.

But The Question haunted me,
Ever present, as I enjoyed the pleasures,
Of embodiment in space and time,
And lost myself in the dream of selfhood,
It whispered, during my agonies and ecstasies…

What happened? Where am I?
What is this?
What is this feeling,
Of existing as "someone".

At thirty-one The Question drove me fiercely,
In search of the Experience I had Known,
Before the swinging of duality's pendulum,
Before I tasted that BitterSweet Apple,
And wandered from The Garden, gasping…

What happened?
Where am I?
What is this?
What is this feeling of existing,
As a stranger in a strange land?

Journeying Within, I found Eden once more,
In the Absolute Vanishing of All dualities,
In the Perfection of Nonexistent Existence,
As That which Exists before the "I" in "I Am",
An Ecstasy, a Rapture, beyond expression.

But returning to the experience of duality,
The mind returned, more confounded than ever,
For I had no knowledge, still, of "truth" or "reality",
But only a second Question, heaped upon the first,
Possessing me from that day forward…

What happened?
What was that Experience of Existing,
In which I, the experiencer, did not exist,
Whose Nature was, as the master said,
The Kingdom of Heaven, Within?

And when I discovered that The Beloved,
Had Returned with me from Heaven,
And taken up Residence in my Heart of Hearts,
I had no knowledge, still, of "what" She was,
But gained only a third Question...

What has happened?
What is this Love, Absolute, without opposite,
This Fullness, Completion, and Ecstasy,
This touch of Heaven's Incomprehensible Rapture,
Here, in this Dream of manifest experience?

Now, at seventy, I remain a Simple man,
Without "knowledge" or "understanding",
Of the Mystery that I Am, before "I" am,
Of the what, when, where, why, and how,
But hear... in each moment... the Call to Prayer...

What was that Nonexistent Existence,
That Fulfillment of the Heart's Desire?
What is this enduring Experience of Grace,
This Radiant Presence, Within?
What... is... This?

In all these many years of questioning,
The Beautiful One has never responded,
With "knowledge" and "understanding",
But each time, instead, Wells Up, Overflowing,
Flooding my Heart, Drowning the questioner.

"Shhh, my Love", She whispers to my Soul,
And as I, the world, and Beloved Vanish, I see,
That there are no words in Heaven,
No names for the Mystery We Are,
And in that Vanishing of all dualities...

No Mystery at all.

THE BEAUTIFUL ONE AWAITS

I grew up soiled by the orthodoxy,
Of the faith in which I was raised,
And all these many decades later,
Have not entirely removed the stain.

For I sometimes awaken confused,
That Love, without cause or opposite,
Fills, Radiant, the Heart of my Being,
While this Simple Cup remains only clay.

A Cup that the orthodox declared,
Must be transmuted through great effort,
Transformed through striving and travail,
Into a golden vessel, worthy of Her Love.

What Blasphemy, what vile Heresy,
Whispered to a small child's spirit,
By the dour jurists of theology,
Enamored of punishment and reward.

In the Garden of the Beloved

They knew nothing, it seems, of Love,
Or the power of Longing to draw Her,
And the Truth, beyond cause and condition,
That She dwells, waiting, in every Heart.

Waiting not for the perfecting of our Being,
Or the accumulation of sufficient merit,
But only for our Heart's Longing to Blossom,
And the Love within us to seek Its Source.

Waiting for Love's Fragrance to capture,
Our outward wandering Attention,
And send it Journeying Inward,
In Search of The Rose.

Waiting for our prodigal fascination,
To turn from the beauty that appears,
To The Beauty within which beauty appears,
Returning Home, to the arms of The Beloved.

Within, where The Beautiful One awaits,
Not distant, transcendent in a far off Heaven,
But as the Light that Illumines our Soul,
As what we Are, before the "I" in "I Am".

Not out there, up there, after, when, or if,
But Now, Here, before time, before space,
In that Placeless Place, that Spaceless Space,
Where, in the Heaven of Nonexistent Existence…

The Beautiful One awaits.

IT'S EACH OF US!

I placed the votive candle,
Into it's beautiful glass holder,
And noted how the frame,
In which the wax was held,
Was so badly bent and battered.

For a moment, I paused, wondering,
Was such a candle fit to light,
In Remembrance of The Beloved,
Framed in such imperfection,
So very far from "worthy".

But lighting the poor fellow I saw,
There, the Radiant Flame,
Perfect and Beautiful in the Center,
Embodied as it was, in form,
Embraced in imperfection.

"It's each of us!" I laughed,
As The Beautiful One Lit my Heart.

AFTER THE FACT

When Attention Rests, Surrendering,
Falling like a wave into the Ocean,
Vanishing like a cloud into the Sky,
Dualities Vanish, as well…

And the naming self is no more.

In that Vanishing is no exclamation,
"Ah... the Self",
"Ah... the Beloved",
"Ah... the formless Absolute"...

"Ah... God".

For when the Namer Vanishes,
When the Interpreter Dies,
When the thinker is no more,
No one, no thing at all, exists to utter...

"Ah..."

No space, no time, no objects,
No subject self to describe "reality",
No "knower" to pronounce the "truth",
No one, no thing at all exists, and yet...

Existence Is... Rapturous, Ecstatic.

Only after the fact, when duality returns,
Does the mind's yammering begin,
Birthed in the Astounded exclamation,
Arising from Inexpressible Awe...

"What... was... That"?!

In the ensuing tsunami of thought,
Nonexistent Existence is made existent,
As The Nameless is named,
The Incomprehensible, described,
The nature of "reality", defined,
The substance of "truth", declared…

After the fact.

Can you forgive me, my friends,
For writing Lovingly of The Beloved,
When neither She nor I have ever existed,
In the Mystery Her Name can only point to…

After the fact.

AND THE DESERT BLOOMED

There was a time when I found myself,
In a Desert where the Dark Night lingered,
And it seemed that the Sun of Hope,
Had set for all eternity.

Despair became for me, the very blood,
That coursed through the veins of my Being,
Hopelessness, the air that I breathed,
Desolation... simply what it felt like to be alive.

In the Garden of the Beloved

The ashes of faith had long blown away,
In arid Winds of Abandonment and Isolation,
And it seemed with a certainty absolute,
That prayers echoed unheard, in Emptiness.

Until one day, at last, Falling where I stood,
I searched through the Ruins of myself,
To find a shard, a crumb, a drop… anything,
That Desolation might have left to me.

And I found, still Glimmering in the ashes,
The flickering Ember of Love's Longing,
That had sent me Journeying, so long ago,
In the quest for its Fulfillment.

A Jewel still Sparkling in that Darkness,
A Tear having withstood the fires of Hell,
A Blessing that Remained, when it seemed,
All Blessings were no more.

Longing had endured, when all hope was lost,
Longing remained, in the ashes of faith,
Longing Shone in that unending Darkness,
Longing alone remained to me.

Longing for Love not born of cause or condition,
A Love for which no opposite existed,
A Love that Shone before this Dream of duality,
In the Heaven of nonexistent Existence.

Holding to my Heart that Jewel of Longing,
Left behind by the Thief of belief and faith,
It was revealed that the Ravager was none other,
Than The Beloved, The Beautiful, The Merciful.

The very Love I had Longed for had driven me,
To the Charnel House of knowledge, belief and faith,
Where the Conflagration of Love's Fierce Flames,
Had Consumed all that Love was not.

In the Ashes, I found the Blessing of Poverty,
For having Nothing, Love's Treasure was Revealed,
Being Nothing, I Existed without existing,
And as the Rains of Heaven began to Fall…

The Desert Bloomed.

THE WALL

There was a time when I pondered,
Building an impenetrable wall, within,
To keep the din and clamor of world and self,
From disturbing the Peace of the Garden,
Where rustling leaves whisper Teachings,
And birdsong Celebrates Her Beauty.

But such effort proved unnecessary,
When The Beautiful One Inhabited my Heart,
And the wall that I alone had ever been,
Was washed away in the Rains of Love,
Until sound and Silence were One,
Movement and Stillness, Undivided.

For True Silence,
Has naught to do with sound,
True Stillness,
Naught to do with movement,
True Love,
Naught to do with condition.

In sound or silence… I Hear Her Voice,
Touching or distant… I Feel Her Warmth,
Moving or still… I Rest in Her Arms,
Blind or sighted… Her Face is before me,
Adored or disdained… Her Love Fills me,
Whatever I may appear to be… I Am.

I continue to attend this heap of rubble,
Watchful for stones that cut and bruise,
Removing what is in my power to remove,
But mindful that the Grace soaked remnants,
Of the wall that I alone had ever been,
Are now the property of The Beloved Architect.

THE TATTERED RUG

I have tender affection,
For rugs with tattered edges,
For I was before, and now remain,
Tattered and torn at the edges,
Even as The Beautiful One,
Inhabits the Heart of my Being.

For Her Radiant Presence,
Has not perfected the whole,
Every aspect of the manifest form,
In a single, Mystical Transmutation,
But weaves Grace, thread by thread,
Stitch by stitch, through warp and woof.

Her Transmuting Alchemy, interwoven,
The Shimmering Filament of Love,
Entwined in the Ultimate of Intimacies,
Into the tattered and soiled fabric,
The inherently imperfect cloth,
Of the manifest Being.

And so, I seek out the tattered rugs,
Deemed unfit for purchase,
By the jurists of religion,
For I, too, have tattered edges,
Which, though appearing as flaws,
Are proof of Love, Unconditional.

For this one, deemed irredeemable,
Was Embraced, and held in Affection,
By The Merciful Weaver of Grace,
Who whispered from within my Heart,
"I am Here for you, Always…"

"My tattered love".

IN HER PRESENCE

Countless tales speak of Love long lost,
Of the enduring pain of separation,
And of Memory lingering in the Heart,
Whispering to the Tragic Lover,
"Do not forget me. I am Here".

Countless tales speak of the Journey,
Of the Lover's long odyssey of Travail,
From the Desert of Forgetfulness,
Through the Wilderness of confusions,
Amidst storms of hopelessness and despair.

They speak of the Wondrous Eventuality,
Of the time-bound Lover falling, in time,
Into the arms of the Timeless Beloved,
And the memory of Separation's Sorrow,
Vanishing, like a mirage suddenly revealed.

Most tales end in this Sweetness,
In the Celebration of Love's Triumph,
In the Glorious Ending of Sorrows,
In the Fulfillment of the Heart's Desire,
As the last page is turned.

But I would add ten thousand pages,
Of how the Story does not end,
Of Living thereafter, in Her Presence,
The ordinary made Extraordinary,
The mundane become Magical.

I would tell of living in space and time,
Of walking, standing, sitting, lying,
Of seeing, hearing, smelling, touching, tasting,
Of "Relative" Subjectivity remaining,
Of "Relative" duality remaining…

In Her Presence.

I would tell of the continuing experience,
Of physicality, psychology, and emotion,
Of perceptions and sensations arising,
Of the river of thought still flowing,
Of our Humanity intact…

In Her Presence.

In the Garden of the Beloved

I would tell of Wonder, Alive and Unquenched,
Of a mind Drenched in Mystery, still searching,
For comprehension of the incomprehensible,
For knowledge of the Unknowable,
For the Grand Conclusion...

In Her Presence.

I would tell how all that was "before", remains,
But Illumined, Transformed, Transmuted,
How on the level of psychology and emotion,
The Alchemy of Refinement continues,
But free of self-judgment and condemnation...

In Her Presence.

I would tell of a Great Relaxation,
The end of concern for Her coming and going,
The end of grasping to hold, in fear of loss,
The certainty, at last, of Her Unending Presence,
And a Sigh that echoes to the Gates of Heaven...

In Her Presence.

THE BELOVED COULD NOT REFUSE

Perhaps it is better that I am imperfect,
So far from sainthood's virtue,
For if the Beautiful One dwells here,
In this ramshackle hut, this crumbling ruin,
Is it not proof for others, imperfect,
Of Love's Unimaginable Grace?

Were I a saint, the jurists would declare,
"But of course She dwells there,
For that temple has become sanctified,
Purified and brought to perfection,
Through a lifetime of spiritual disciplines,
And rigorous adherence to the "law".

But it has not been so.

As it is, they are left scratching their heads,
For bound in legality, they cannot conceive,
How Love would transcend the rule of law,
And convey a beggar, poor in perfection,
But Rich with Longing and Sincerity,
To this Table, set by the Cup Bearer.

They cannot conceive that when I cried,
With the Whole of my imperfect Being,
For a Love beyond cause or condition,
Beyond prerequisite or requirement,
Beyond perfection and imperfection,
A Love beyond all dualities…

The Beloved could not refuse.

I KNOW A SIMPLE ONE

You do not have to believe this or that,
To Experience Love's Inner Radiance,
For I know one who questions everything,
Whose Heart is Aglow in that Light.

You need not have faith in this or that,
To be Held in the Divine Embrace,
For I know a doubter, living in Unknowing,
Whose head rests upon Her lap.

You need not be holy to see a Vision,
Of the Beautiful Mystery Revealed,
For I know a simple one, far from holiness,
Who Received Her Loving Gaze.

You need not be perfected in virtue,
To Receive Love without cause or condition,
For I know a simple one, far from Perfection,
Who Breathes Love in and out.

You need not feel the body an impediment,
Obscuring, obstructing, hindering,
For I know a simple one whose flesh and blood,
Is imbued with Love's Formless Ecstasy.

You need not have keen intellect,
To gain Wisdom beyond knowledge,
For I know a simple one of hobbled mind,
Who Knows what cannot be known.

A simple one, flawed, wounded, broken,
Relishing the pleasures of body and world,
Petulant, rebellious, and obstinate,
Weak-willed and undisciplined...

Who Loved Her with Heart and Soul,
Who ached with the whole of Being,
Who shed tears of Longing, again and again,
Who collapsed, and did not rise...

Who, crying out, was Embraced,
Crying out, was Illumined,
Crying out, was Freed,
Crying out... was Loved.

To each a nature is given,
From each nature a Path unfolds,
And no law, spiritual or temporal,
Can bind the Hand of the Beloved's Grace.

How do I know this?

I know a simple one.

WHAT IS IT LIKE?

There are many transient experiences,
"States" experienced along The Way,
Which, although coming and going,
Become, in passing, a part of our totality.

Like a sudden rain of Benediction,
Showering Grace upon our wilted spirit,
Such are these transient states,
Refreshing, renewing, inspiring.

Some rue their ephemeral nature,
And in their passing, deem them "gone",
But their Waters only appear to have dried,
Sunken deep within our Roots.

There are "stations", as well, along the Way,
Enduring Transmutations of our Being,
No longer coming and going,
Having become inherent in our experience.

Like the Sudden cracking of a green bud,
Revealing petals formerly hidden,
Never again a seed, never again a bud,
An event in time, as the Timeless Blossoms.

I smile at the implication of finality,
In words like enlightenment and awakening,
For no matter the profundity of one's station,
"Enlightening", as I see it, is an endless affair.

The Mystic Poets use the word Love,
To describe the longing that moves us,
And That to which our longing aspires,
For longing is "of" That which is longed for.

And although Love is a word so entwined,
With romantic, embodied connotation,
Even so, when we read the Poet Lovers,
It is our Souls that leap in Recognition.

In Recognition, Remembrance, Knowing,
More Intimate than any other,
An Ancient Memory of Something Known,
But somehow, along the Way, forgotten.

A whisper, from the depths of our Soul,
A still, small voice, Beckoning, Reminding,
Of Existence before duality's arising,
As our Essence, in the Ecstasy of Heaven.

But when our Essence, Alive but unmanifest,
Shines into our manifest Experience,
It brings to this Dream of dualities,
A masala* of qualities, an advieh* of attributes.

You Feel Loved,
Wholly, Completely, Absolutely,
In a way you could not have conceived,
But... no one is there, Loving you.

In the Garden of the Beloved

You Feel Held,
Not in imagination, but tangibly,
Embraced, enfolded, enveloped,
And yet… no one is there, holding you.

You Feel Richness and Warmth,
Filling your Experience, within and without,
No matter the ever-changing nature,
Of that which appears without, or arises within.

You Feel Fullness and Completion,
In the Deepest Interiority of your Being,
Unmoving, Impenetrable, Absolute,
The end of lack, and grasping for "more".

You no longer feel "your" self,
Though all that defined "you" remains,
Unowned, in a space now Serene and Empty,
But Full, of Exquisite, Vibrant Aliveness.

You feel Bliss, a touch of Union's Ecstasy,
Ever Shining without center or periphery,
That when Rested into, carries you away,
Into the Ecstasy of Dissolution.

Radiant, as well, in the Heart of Being,
Is Fathomless Gratitude and Appreciation,
For the Experience of manifest existence,
For the Kingdom of Heaven, Within.

However futile it may seem to reason,
You cannot help but Pray with each breath,
For the end of all suffering,
Everywhere, Now, and forever.

You Feel Affection for all that appears,
In the Dream of manifest existence,
A Tender Hearted but Fierce Desire,
For the Happiness, the Rightness, of All That Is.

You Feel yourself in Intimate Relationship,
With this Incomprehensible Mystery,
And are ever in communion and dialog,
In the wordless language of The Heart.

Like Attar, You no longer know anything,
No longer understand anything,
You feel yourself so Deeply in Love,
But with whom, with what, you do not know.

Like Rumi, you no longer know who you are,
The Beloved having woven Herself,
So Intimately into the fabric of your Being,
That you live in Astounded, Lucid, Confusion.

Like Ibn Arabi, yours is the religion of Love,
And wherever you come upon its Sweetness,
In mosque, temple, church, or tavern,
There is your belief, the faith you hold.

In the Garden of the Beloved

Like Hafez, and "every sane person he knows",
You have jumped overboard from the ship,
Of binding orthodoxy and shackling dogma,
Into the lifeboat of the Poet, the Lover.

You have become as a Mad Dervish,
Wandering the Wilderness of The Unknown,
Cherishing Experience above ideology,
Dancing, where dancing is forbidden.

Your Life is a Play of Mystical Delight,
In which the Player upon the stage,
Is ever Enfolded in the Loving Light,
Of The Director's Gaze.

You are a Wave no longer separate,
Dancing upon, and as, the Ocean of Bliss,
In which the tides of life's ecstasies and agonies,
Ebb and flow in the Mystery that You Are.

You lay no claim to "Perfection",
For only The Beautiful One is so,
And pointing, always, from your face to Hers,
Rest in Her Perfecting Grace.

You cry more often than "before",
But tears of a different nature,
For the Heartrending Suffering of Creation,
And its Breathtaking, Rapturous Beauty.

Do you see why it is called madness?
Do you see why it is called Intoxication?
Do you see why it is called the Beloved?
Do you see why it is called Love?

Everyone's path is unique,
Everyone's experience their own,
But on the Path of Love and Surrender,
That I have been Blessed to follow…

This is what it is like.

* Spice mixtures in Indian and Persian cuisine, respectively.

OUT HERE

I like it out here, where no one can see,
Far from any notion of myself.
Here, I am no one, and yet, I Am.

Out here I am Unclothed.
Can you imagine the Delight,
Leaving that scratchy garment behind?

Out here no intercessor stands,
Between the arising and the arisen,
Between Heaven and Earth.

Out here I am far away,
From the raucous din and clamor,
Of the spiritual bazaar.

In the Garden of the Beloved

"Shhh!" We don't debate out here,
Where "Truth" is a word,
In a land where no language is spoken.

Out here I care nothing,
For what others think of what I think,
For I care nothing of what I think.

Out here thought and feeling arise,
Only thinker and feeler are lost,
And the River Flows, undammed.

What Rapture, out here,
Where I Exist without existing,
In the Answer to every Prayer ever uttered.

What a Blessing to discover,
Out here,
In Here.

One more thing, lest you misunderstand,
The mind still seeks, as is its nature,
To comprehend the Incomprehensible,
But Surrendered, long ago, to Not Knowing.

WHY?

Why would I journey far, to Holy places,
When the Heart's Desire is Fulfilled, Here?
If I craved more of Her, I would surely move,
But I cannot, Fullness having stilled my Soul.

When I journey to places of Holiness,
It is because The Beloved, Resting Here,
Lifts Herself from Her Sublime Repose,
Desiring to Dance in the company of Lovers.

Why would I read further to learn more,
Studying descriptions of the indescribable,
When the Alpha and Omega, wordlessly,
Teaches from the depths of my Heart?

I read because the mind, now a Drunken Fool,
Derives such sweet Intoxication and Joy,
From the Drops She Graciously allows to spill,
From the Cup of Incomprehensibility.

Why would I deem any place Dear or Holy,
When my Soul circles the Ka'ba of my Heart,
The Beloved Shining so Brightly, there,
That I am Blinded to Holy and unholy?

I deem a place Dear and Holy when,
Like a babe in The Mother's Womb,
My Soul kicks in Joyful Recognition,
Of The Beautiful One, embodied there.

The Mother of Mercy has woven Herself,
Into the Fabric of my Heart, mind, and Soul,
So that turning within, in Remembrance of Her,
I find, at the end of my self and all things…

I Am.

This does not glorify the earthen vessel,
As the orthodox legalists would accuse,
But the Wine within, Poured by the Cup Bearer,
Seeping, through Grace, into the clay.

For the Soul of every being is in Essence, Divine,
And journeying from the far frontiers of Heaven,
All may Return, and enter, at last, the Heart,
Vanishing, in the Inner Sanctum of The Beloved.

For all these questions, only one answer…

Love.

THE ROSE UNSEEN

I find it difficult to discard,
Plants which are near to death,
Fading, whatever the cause may be,
For I, too, was once near death,
Saved only by the Beloved Gardener.

The legalists, the jurists of religion,
Would have tossed my Soul aside,
Onto the heap of the irredeemable,
Deeming further care a waste of Water,
My Being far too ravaged by Drought.

But a Loving Eye fell upon me,
And a Heart of Grace was moved,
To Embrace, with Merciful Hands,
The starving root and withered branch,
Of my near breathless Soul.

'Twas the Beautiful One who moved me,
From the broken pot of my self,
And placed me into the Ground of Being,
In the Secret Garden of Her Heart,
Tending me there, with Living Waters.

These days, though that which is visible,
Appears to wilt and wither with age,
Within, beyond the touch of time,
A Rose, unseen, is ever in Bloom,
Surrounding me with Her Perfume.

I find it difficult to discard,
Those encountered along The Way,
In whom root and branch are suffering,
And hold them in Prayerful Affection,
For I, too, would be discarded…

Were it not for the Beloved Gardener.

IN THIS DREAM OF MANIFEST
EXISTENCE

In the Ecstasy of Your Embrace, dualities Vanish,
For there is no space in which objects might appear,
No duration of time, in which they might be perceived,
And Vanished, as well, the subject perceiver.

Neither Thou nor I exist, and yet... I Am.

But here... in this Dream of manifest existence,
You are the space within which the world and I appear,
For all that I am, all that I know, arises within You,
Knower, known, knowing; all movements of Your breath.

Here... in this Dream of manifest existence,
You are the River of Time, within which Creation flows,
For birth, growth, maturation, decay, and death,
Like clouds, appear and vanish within You.

Here... in this Dream of manifest existence,
You are all that Appears within space and time,
This Vehicle of Perception, and all that is perceived,
Perceiver, perceived, perceiving; Your heartbeat.

Here... in this Dream of manifest existence,
You are the Longing which moved my Weary Heart,
An Ancient Memory, crying from the depths of my Soul,
For a Love once Known, then... somehow... forgotten.

Here… in this Dream of manifest existence,
You are the Unimaginable Fulfillment of that Longing,
The Answer to every prayer ever uttered, in all of Creation,
That Ancient Love once Known… Known again.

You are the choreographer of this dance of dualities,
The playwright of this Mystery of Longing and Fulfillment,
The Radiant Unmanifest, Illumining the manifest stage,
Shining in our Deepest Interiority, Behind… Before… As…

This Dream of manifest existence.

ALL ELSE… FORGOTTEN

I have never been able to still my mind,
To quiet the incessant inner chatter,
Or quell its frenetic energies,
Through the use of will,
Or understanding,
Or technique.

'Twas Love and Longing that freed me,
From the mind's gravity, the self's inertia.
My inner Gaze so fixed upon Her Face,
That all else became simply… forgotten,
Mind and senses unheard, unseen, unfelt.

In the Garden of the Beloved

Hearing only the Music of Her Silent voice,
Smelling only the Fragrance of Her Perfume,
Tasting only the Sweetness of Her Wine,
Seeing only the Radiance of Her Face,
Feeling only the Warmth of Her Presence.

Love was the River that carried this Ulysses,
Past the enchanting sirens of the mind,
Its Current rending the garment self,
Until the naked Soul drowned,
In the Ocean of its Essence.

On this Path of Love and Surrender,
The discipline to be marshaled is Love,
The technique to be mastered is Surrender,
The understanding to be gained is Poverty,
All but The Beautiful One, simply… Forgotten.

And what is this "Beloved", so Adored?
'Tis the Feeling of your Self, before your self,
The Essence at the Heart of your Being,
Where Lover and Beloved Embrace,
Where, before "I" and "Thou"…

I Am.

THE PRICE OF LOVE

Whether I feast or abstain, enjoy or refrain,
Neither is the cause of Her Loving Presence,
Gracing the Heart of this Drunkard,
From a placeless place, beyond dualities.

Performing rituals or daydreaming idly,
Neither is a price paid for Grace,
For this Garland cannot be purchased,
Or bartered for with deeds fulfilled.

This Ecstasy has no cause but Love,
No demand of prerequisites fulfilled,
That lesser love requires be made,
In monies of fear and desire.

The greatest Heartbreak in Creation,
Is the lie devised by heartless legalists,
That The Beautiful One, The Merciful,
Holds forth Love… for a price.

And yet, I recall a distant time,
Before She inhabited my Broken Heart,
When I cried with Desperate Longing,
And ached, with the Whole of my Being.

And so, perhaps, there is a price for Love,
Paid from the coffers of our Heart,
A dowry that turns The Beloved's Face,
Drawing Love to our Longing.

But Lovers, do not despair of your fate,
For The Bountiful One has Filled your Hearts,
With Treasure sufficient to the cost,
For the Price of Love…

Is Love.

NOT QUITE HERE, NOT QUITE THERE

In the realm of here and there,
I am here, The Beloved, there.
In the Realm of The Heart,
There is no space.

In the realm of now and then,
Paradise is a distant dream.
In the Realm of The Heart,
There is no time.

In the realm of this and that,
She is Beloved, and I, Lover.
In the Realm of The Heart,
There are no objects.

In the realm of cause and effect,
Each cause has an effect.
In the Realm of The Heart,
There are no such dualities.

When the Realm of The Heart,
Shines into the realm of dualities,
The mind becomes… Blurry,
The Heart Filled with Ecstasy.

The secular becomes sacred,
The mundane, magical,
The ordinary, extraordinary,
The imperfect, immaculate.

And one finds one's self,
Even in the midst of infinite space,
Even in the midst of eternal time,
Even in the midst of myriad objects…

Not quite here, not quite there.

THE COMPASS OF MY SOUL

I've read so much of the Great Paths,
Resonating here, with this aspect,
Uneasy there, with that,
Until, setting those tomes aside…

'Twas You I found, oh Book of my Heart.

I've traveled to see famed teachers,
Uplifted here, by this one,
Disturbed there, by that one,
Until, leaving those places…

'Twas You I found, oh Font of Grace.

I've sojourned in the villages of faith,
Discovering precious jewels,
Midst the rubbled heaps of dogma,
But always, washing away the mud…

'Twas You I found there, Sparkling.

Beyond the safe harbors of orthodoxy,
In deep waters of The Great Mystery,
Tossed in Dread Tempests of Unknowing,
Unanchored, Rudderless, Adrift…

'Twas You I found, the Compass of my Soul.

THE BEAUTIFUL ROOMMATE

How could I ever forget the day I discovered,
The Beloved had returned with me from Heaven,
And against all that religious jurists declare,
Had taken up Residence in my Heart.

But since that day, when Grace was made manifest,
It has not been easy for all who inhabit this House,
Most tragically for our roommate, the mind,
For She refuses to speak in his language.

"This is not helpful!" he turned to me, frustrated.

In spite of relentless enquiries,
She will not reveal to the poor fellow,
In any way comprehensible to intellect,
The Who, What, When, Where, Why of Herself.

"This is not helpful!" he turned to me, distraught.

And I have fared little better in all of this,
For without asking, She has gone through my things,
Tossing traditions long held in reverence,
Breaking beliefs into tiny pieces, unrecognizable…

Leaving the mess for me to clean up.

When I asked if She might relent briefly,
Or help, at the least, in cleaning the mess,
The Incomprehensible Mystery left in Her Wake,
She Kissed my Heart, and I Fainted in Ecstasy.

"This is not helpful", the mind bemoaned.

For reasons that remain a Mystery,
She left a piece of Faith intact upon the mantle,
But when I asked what this Faith might be for,
She Kissed my Heart, and I Fainted in Ecstasy.

"This is not helpful", the mind sighed.

When Her Presence Filled this House,
I fled for respite, locking myself in my Room,
But found Her there, within myself, as my very Soul,
And overwhelmed by Her Beauty, Fainted in Ecstasy.

"I Surrender", the mind whispered, Swooning.

Had I foreseen what would befall this House,
How in handing The Beloved the Key to my Heart,
She would Destroy these walls, and all within,
Leaving this Illumined Ruin...

I would have Fainted in Ecstasy.

SOMETHING... WONDERFUL

I can't remember when it all began, so long ago,
The sudden awareness of existing in space and time,
The earliest arisings of sensation and perception.
Alas, my first memories are years after that big bang.

I can't remember when awareness of myself arose,
In that Field of Perception without center or periphery,
The felt sense of "I", separate, isolated, alone,
When the reed was cut from soil and water.

I can't remember when language was learned,
And thereafter wrapped all of experience,
Cloaking nameless, formless Wonder,
In words, concepts, and mental imagery.

I can't remember when it first arose...
The relentless concern over stature, self-esteem,
Am I attractive, desirable, respected, admired,
And most viciously cruel; am I worthy of love.

I don't remember when the Suffering of life,
Born of both human cruelty and Nature's wrath,
Breached the walls of my unsuspecting heart,
And engendered an ever-present, ambient sorrow.

Ever so slowly I wandered into the Desert of Estrangement,
Unaware of the gradual obscuration and contraction,
Falling ever more deeply asleep, ever more deeply lost,
In a dream of myself, myself, myself, and the world.

Hell.

But I do remember, when the pain became too great,
Fleeing so very deeply within, in search of that Essential Me,
Existent before all that had accrued, after the fact,
Of qualities and attributes defining Peripheral me.

I remember when, Journeying in search of my ending,
I found The Beginningless Beginning of myself and all that Is,
And Vanishing there as myself, along with all that is,
Remained Alive… as the Essence of Life Itself.

I remember the Ecstasy of that Nonexistent Existence,
For which there are no analogs in manifest experience,
An Ecstasy experienced in the Vanishing of the experiencer,
The Absolute Fulfillment of the Heart's Desire.

Heaven.

And I remember that when I and the world reappeared,
The Ecstasy of Heaven, before "I" and the world ever were,
Returned with me to manifest Existence in space and time,
A Divine stowaway in the Heart of Being.

And I remember how The Beloved resided, thereafter,
As a Wellspring of Dissolution and Bliss in The Heart,
Her Tavern, Her Garden, the Soul's Light Shining,
Nonexistent Existence, here... in the midst of existence.

Heaven on earth.

I remember how the Sorrows of manifest existence continued,
Even as the Soul's Sorrowless Light Illumined Experience,
And how those Sorrows and the Soul's Ecstasy, co-existing,
Became... something else.

And I remember how the individuated self continued,
Even as the Soul's Selfless Light Illumined Experience,
And how individuated self and Selfless Soul, co-existing,
Became... something else.

Something... Wonderful.

THE NAVIGATOR'S PLIGHT

The mind said to the Heart…

"I'm the navigator,
Here in the passenger's seat,
Map spread open on my lap,
Reason and logic plotting the route,
Looking up only now and then,
To point frantically,
'No! This way!'"

"You, alas, dear Heart, are driving,
Intoxicated, dancing in your seat,
Swerving all over The Road,
Sometimes turning as I direct,
Other times, ignoring me entirely,
Lost in a daydream of Her Face,
And yet… somehow… Magically…

We arrive".

YEARNING

Have you never held your Beloved,
As closely as embrace allows,
And not felt, still, within that deepest intimacy,
Longing's Bittersweet Ache, enduring?

In the Garden of the Beloved

I have known The Heaven of Union,
Where I, She, and all things Vanished,
And in the Absolute Fulfillment of all Longing,
Only Unspeakable Ecstasy remained.

And when the world and I reappeared,
From that Heaven that Is, before all that is,
The Gate to the Secret Garden remained open,
The door to the Tavern of The Beloved, ajar.

Thereafter, although no longer Vanished in Eden,
I experienced a River flowing from that Paradise,
Into the Wellspring of the Heart,
Here, in this Dream of manifest existence.

And yet... I Yearn.

I live each moment with Yearning,
Each heartbeat,
Each breath,
The most Beautiful Ache.

Even in the midst of a Blessed life,
I still gaze off, wistfully, dreamily,
Distracted by Her Perfume, Her Nearness,
And the Memory of Heaven.

When I speak of Her, of The Beloved,
I speak of both that Heaven, before Creation,
And the Presence of Heaven's Ecstasy,
That inhabits my Heart here, in Creation.

How then can I Yearn, if the Wellspring of my Heart,
Is Filled to overflowing with Her Love,
And the Rose Blooms Fragrant, Intoxicating,
In The Secret Garden, within?

How can I say that all is Fulfilled,
When Longing endures, ever present,
Coloring each of time's precious moments,
With the BitterSweet hues of Desire?

I can only answer in Contradictions,
That although Her Love Fills my Heart, I Yearn,
That although Heaven Shines within, I Ache,
That although Ecstasy takes my breath, I cry.

For however much "I" have Diminished,
However much She Fills the space where "I" had been,
However much the boundaries,
Of Heaven and Earth have Vanished…

Yearning's Beauty is inherent in Love's Fulfillment.

VEILS

So many names for, so many descriptions of, The Mystery.

The name I cherish most dearly is Wordless, Unspeakable,
The only description my weary mind can accept, Unknowable,
All names, all descriptions being…

So many Veils.

And yet, when the heart speaks of the Unspeakable,
It uses names… "Beloved", "Beautiful One", "My Own",
Knowing full well that these expressions of Love are…

So many Veils.

And when the mind seeks in vain to describe the Unknowable,
It uses metaphors… "Friend", "Teacher", "Guide",
Knowing full well that these expressions of Wisdom are…

So many Veils.

What is it that is Veiled by names, however Beautiful,
Veiled by descriptions, metaphor, however Humbled and Wise,
Veiled by all that appears, and… by we to whom all appears?

You'll have to ask your Heart.

THE GREAT ROBBERY

The Beloved broke in while I slept,
And wherever in this House She found,
Knowledge, belief, and certitude,
She stole them, quietly, deftly,
Leaving Wonder where they had been.

The mind deemed this robbery a tragedy,
And ran, frantically, to check those places,
Where its treasures had been displayed,
Only to find, in their place, Great Mysteries,
Gifts of Love, from the Divine Thief.

The Heart deemed the robbery a Blessing,
And cause for the greatest celebration,
Running, straightaway, to The Tavern,
Where, in the company of The Thief,
Its Cup of Longing was Filled with Her Wine.

And in time the mind came 'round,
And resigned at last to Poverty,
Joined the Jubilant Heart at The Bar,
Drinking all The Beautiful One would pour,
Into its now Empty Cup.

And together they reveled, Heart and Mind,
In the Great Gift the Robbery had bestowed,
The Divine Idiocy of Direct Experience,
Before words and concepts arise to describe,
When Heart and Mind Dance in the Ecstasy…

Of Astounded, Lucid, Confusion.

WATERLOGGED

It is not in the waters of knowledge that I Drown,
It is The Ocean of The Unknown into which "I" sink,
Its waters Dissolving, with each inhale,
All that I have come to know of "reality",
All that I have felt "myself" to be.

I understand the need,
To give a name to,
To ascribe an image for,
To imbue with relatable persona,
The Nameless… Formless… Mystery.

For like all who face the Incomprehensible,
The Whole of my Being shuddered
Watching the exhausted mind,
Clutch desperately at understanding,
As the Tsunami of Unknowing swept it away.

It could not grasp the Unfathomable Mystery,
That we appear in this Dream of space,
Endure, for a time, in the Dream of time,
And then, as with all things manifest,
Vanish into Nonexistent Existence.

Call The Beautiful One by any name,
And if you must, explain reality,
But this Drunkard has fallen overboard,
Washed up on the Shore of The Unknowable,
Waterlogged with Wonder, Dripping Love.

THE MIND STILL WONDERS

Oh, the mind still wonders,
About the unfathomable mystery of life,
Even though the Whole of Being,
Is Drunk on The Beloved's Wine.

It still revels in contemplation about,
In deep consideration of,
In profound meditation upon,
But now… like an enchanted child.

Oh, it still desires to know,
But no longer "struggles" to do so,
No longer "needs" as it did, before,
The fruition of concept and theory.

For The Question has been Answered,
Not in thought, word, or concept,
Not in knowledge or understanding,
For nothing is known, nothing understood.

The Question has been answered,
In the Living Presence, Here, in form,
Of the Soul's formless Ecstasy Revealed,
Shining in dualities, beyond dualities.

And still… the mind Wonders.

IN THE AUTUMN OF LIFE

In the Autumn of life…
I no longer care for "knowledge of",
In words, concepts, and theories,
For the highest knowledge possible,
Remains but yet another veiling.

And yet...
The mind continues as it has,
Reveling in its noble quest,
Behaving according to its nature,
Only now, knowing full well the futility.

In the Autumn of life...
I no longer care for "understanding",
Arriving at a logical "conclusion",
For the deepest understanding possible,
Remains but yet another veiling.

And yet...
The mind continues as it has,
Devouring whatever crumbs might fall,
From the Table of The Great Mystery,
Only now, knowing full well the futility.

In the Autumn of life...
I care only for this Inner Radiance,
The Ecstasy of the Soul, Revealed,
Rich, Warm, Vibrant, Alive,
Here, now, in The Heart of Being.

And yet, in the Autumn of life...
I see this Blessing is born of our entirety,
The mind's desperate need to Know,
The Heart's desperate desire to Feel,
The Soul's desperate longing for Union.

The Sunlight of the mind's Light,
Warmed the Earth of the Heart's Longing,
And Living Waters Showering from the Soul,
Nourished, gave birth to, and Blossomed,
This Benediction of Causeless Love…

Here… in the Autumn of life.

HERE, IN THIS WORLD

I attend to so many things,
As we all must do each day,
Caring for the "outer" garden,
Moving about in this Dream,
In which the world exists,
And "I" within it.

Adding and subtracting,
Doing this, doing that,
Going here, going there,
Learning, developing skills,
To sustain my existence,
In this manifest creation.

But don't think for an instant,
That in all of this busy "outwardness",
The Beloved is not Here in the midst,
Like the air surrounding this body,
The space in which I move,
The blood within these veins.

In the Garden of the Beloved

Though this world and I arise within Her,
She is Here, as well, within the arisen,
Within this world, within me,
Making the secular, Sacred,
The ordinary, Extraordinary,
The mundane, Magical.

If you think this Grace has come,
By dint of saintly virtue,
Through disciplined practice,
The mastery of technique,
Or refinement of the self,
Nothing could be further from truth.

This Grace came about,
Because the Love that She is,
The Love that I Am,
The Love that you Are,
Has no cause in conditionality,
But Shines, inherent in our Soul.

Journeying within,
I discovered the Essence of my Being,
And there, within, the Essence of Hers.
And that Union, in which She and I Vanish,
Filled this imperfect vessel, thereafter,
With the Perfection of Her Presence...

Here... in this world.

IF YOU COME FOR TEA

If you come for tea and sweets, my Muslim friend,
Don't leave in a huff if you see upon my wall,
The picture of a Hindu Goddess smiling.

If you come to sit in fellowship, my Christian friend,
Don't curl your lip at the Moorish lanterns,
The books of Hafez, Sanai, and Attar strewn about.

If you come for the porch's soft breeze, my Buddhist friend,
Don't dismiss me as a deluded deist when tears well up,
As I gaze at the Christian monstrance.

My house, my Heart, my Life,
Is a Wine of many grapes, but One Vintner,
A Garden of many Roses, but One Gardener.

"I profess the religion of Love", said Ibn Arabi,
"Wherever its caravan turns along the way,
That is the belief, the faith I keep".

And so it will be with you and me,
My friends of many faiths,
If you come for tea.

WATER TO WINE

The magic ingredient,
To turn the tepid water,
Of intellectual "knowledge",
Of cerebral "understanding",
And logical "conclusion",
Into the Intoxicating Wine,
Of Direct Experience...

Is Love.

If you don't yet have it,
In the pantry of your Being,
Leave the mind, locking it behind you,
And bringing with you an empty cup,
Go to the Market of Wonder,
To the Stall of Surrender,
And tell the Vendor of Humility...

That Unbearable Longing has sent you.

MAKING TROUBLE

In the Vanishing that is Union,
There are no words,
No exclamations of "Rapture!"

No one is there to exclaim,
No other there to hear,
And thus... Rapture!

No words, no thought,
Not even the subtle presence,
Of wordless recognition.

For no one is there to recognize,
The "recognizer" having Vanished,
Leaving only... Experience.

Experience of what, by what,
When "what" no longer exists,
And only Heaven remains?

No longer Heaven, "within",
For like All else that was,
Within and without have Vanished.

Ah, and then that Moment,
When the Vanished returns,
As space, time, world, and self.

When the thinker begins thinking,
About the Experience of not existing,
Somehow, impossibly, "Remembering".

This is when the trouble begins!

The Indescribable, described,
In countless words and concepts,
By one who was... not there.

But, what is one to do,
Having found Water in the Desert,
But make trouble, pointing desperately…

Within!

FORGETTING… REMEMBERING

I don't sit in a certain posture, hands held thus.
I forget the body, and the one who would inhabit it.

I don't breathe in a certain way.
I forget breath, and the one who would breathe.

I don't hear a certain sound.
I forget hearing, and the one who would hear.

I don't speak certain words.
I forget language, and the one who would speak.

I don't focus here or there, or imagine certain things.
I forget sight, and the one who would see.

I don't think certain thoughts.
I forget thinking, and the one who would think.

I don't believe certain beliefs.
I forget beliefs, and the one who would believe.

I forget all that is experienced,
And the one who would experience it.

And when at last the one who would Remember is Forgotten,
Remembrance remains, of what remains.

And what Remains…
What remains… is…

Heaven.

EYES OPEN, HERE IN THIS WORLD

There are moments when the last thing I want,
Is to close my eyes and journey within,
For in these moments of Grace,
Within and without have lost all meaning,
And this Vehicle of Perception, and all Perceived,
Are Illumined by the Light of The Soul…

The Light of The Beloved,
Eyes open, here in this world.

In these moments I do not Long for Heaven,
And care nothing for the nonexistence of Union,
Concerning myself with self-perfecting,
For in these moments of Grace…

All is Fulfilled,
Eyes open, here in this world.

 In the Garden of the Beloved

In these moments of Grace,
Heaven is Here, Now, Everywhere,
In the Dream of existence in space and time,
And the Ecstasy of Union's Perfection,
Shines like a Sun in the Heart of Being...

Illumining the dualities of manifest Creation,
Eyes open, here in this world.

In these moments of Grace,
All notions of Holiness and unholiness,
Thoughts of worthiness and unworthiness,
Of The Merciful One's Love being conditional,
All such hellish dualities, Vanished...

And Love's True Meaning, Revealed,
Eyes open, here in this world.

What prayer is there to utter wordlessly,
Whispered with every breath,
Moving as every heartbeat?
"Let each moment be a moment of Grace,
For Everyone, Everywhere, Now, and Forever...

Eyes open, here in this world".

SHE WHISPERED

A voice said…
"For you, of all people, there is no hope,
Of experiencing The Beloved's Embrace,
For scripture declares, She cannot touch the 'unclean'",

And She whispered…
"Your tears have washed away clean and unclean".

A voice said…
"For you, of all people, there is no possibility,
Of surrender, of vanishing in Union beyond dualities,
For you are shackled, bound in servitude to your self'".

And She whispered…
"The key of Unbearable Longing has freed you".

A voice said…
"Of all Hearts, yours can never be,
The dwelling place of The Beautiful, The Radiant One,
For Her Perfection cannot abide in such corruption".

And She whispered…
"Your Heart, Surrendered in Love, has made you Holy to me".

So many voices have spoken…
So many words, with firm authority, citing scriptures,
Words that break the Heart, and wound the spirit,
"She will Love you only if, only when, only after".

And She whispered…

"These legalists know nothing of Love".

Whispering again…
She made vanish the one who would be judged,
And left the remnants of that imperfect self,
Filled with Her Perfume.

ETERNAL, INFINITE, COUNTLESS

I do not use the word "eternal" when speaking of Union,
For eternal is endless time, here in the Dream of existence,
And in the Nonexistent Existence of Her Embrace,
There is no time.

What word to use for Timeless Existence?

I do not use the word "infinite", when speaking of Union,
For infinite is endless space, here in the Dream of existence,
And in the Nonexistent Existence of Her Face,
There is no space.

What word to use for Spaceless Existence?

If I use the word "Beloved", when speaking of Union,
I do not mean an "object" of Love, in the Dream of existence. For
in the Nonexistent Existence of Vanishing in Her Eyes,
There are no objects.

What word to use for Formless Existence?

Birth, growth, maturation, decay, and death,
Here, there, near, far, to and from,
This and that, I and thou,
All are of this Dream…

Where words describe the describable.

"She", "Beloved", "Embrace", "Eyes", "Vanishing",
Are but a Drunken man's finger, lifted, shaking,
Pointing to Nowhere, to Never, to Nothing,
To Nonexistent Existence…

To Heaven, beyond all dualities.

A LITTLE TRICKLE

When "I" drowned in The Ocean,
From which all that appears, appears,
There was no duality whatsoever,
Yet "I" Remember Existing, Nonexistent.

How can "I" Remember, when "I" was not?

It can only be that "I Am", even when "I" am not,
Though "what" I Am remains a Mystery.
For in that Heaven of Nonexistent Existence,
Who, what, when, where, why, and how did not exist.

Are not all words that follow the unfollowable, folly?

In any case, such questions hold no allure.
I leave them to the jurists and theologians,
Who delight in describing "reality", and law,
Creating "believers", and endless strife.

The only matter of consequence to "me",
Is that even as "I" exist in this Dream of form,
"I Am" Shines Formless, still, in the Heart,
A little trickle, a Stream from Heaven Flowing…

From "I Am", into, and as, "I".

And the mind rushes in…
How can "into" and "as" both be true?
How can the Soul be "of" God, yet distinct?
How many angels fit on the head of a pin?

I can only struggle to convey,
That which can never be conveyed,
That where The Kingdom of Heaven ends,
And "I" begin, can no longer be discerned.

A Little Trickle flowing, each drop, The Ocean.

When you weary of dogma and belief,
The Great Question, "What am I"? will drive you,
Within, past all that mind and senses present,
Past even the questioning "I"…

To the Kingdom of Heaven, the "Am" before "I Am".

And upon your Return to this Dream of existence,
I pray you, too, will have poked a hole in Heaven,
And the Light of "Am" will Shine, Illuminating "I",
Brightening the Hearts of all you meet upon The Way.

A little Light, a little Beam Shining, all colors in One.

GO WHERE THE WATER IS

Go where the Water is!
Enough of gazing, parched,
At pictures of The Oasis,
At words describing Wetness.

Where is this Living Water?
Within!

Journey to The Kingdom!
Enough of studying maps,
Moving your finger to follow routes,
Printed on a page, going nowhere.

Where is this Kingdom of Heaven?
Within!

Find The Treasure of Love!
Enough pawning your Heart,
For the trinket of conditional love.
Become the Love that Shines causeless.

Where is this Causeless Love?
Within!

And yet… no admonitions will move,
One infatuated with the outer,
Still reveling in words, concepts, images,
"About" the Face of The Beloved.

No fiery encouragements will rouse,
One besotted with "knowledge",
Mistaking the water of understanding,
For the Wine of Experience.

Should you find yourself thus abstracted,
Unable to awaken from your reverie,
Do not make an anguish of it,
Only rest, sweet Dreamer.

Slumber, untroubled, until such time,
As The Troubler of Hearts shakes you,
And Guides your drowsy steps,
To the Fulfillment of your Heart's Desire…

Where the Water is.

IN SHA' ALLAH

I've no doubt I will die in Wonder,
The mind having collapsed along The Way,
Under the weight of Not Knowing.

What I will most surely not do is die,
Covered by the soil of belief and dogma.

In sha' Allah.

I've no doubt I will die Loving,
No longer seeking to give and receive,
Having become Love Itself.

What I will most surely not do is die,
Wondering if I have "earned" Her Embrace.

In sha' Allah.

I've no doubt I will die Surrendered,
Having released my grip on the rudder,
Adrift upon the Ocean of Grace.

What I will most surely not do,
Is die struggling to be the captain.

In sha' Allah.

I've no doubt that when I die,
"I" will have long since vanished,
In the arms of The Beautiful One.

What I will most surely not do,
Is die Alone, as myself.

In sha' Allah.

May we all Live, Here, Now,
Even as we will Die, There, Then,
Enfolded in Mercy, Compassion, and Grace.

In sha' Allah.

AFTER

After The Beloved Filled my Heart...

I read that tears would never again fall,
But they did, for the suffering of this world,
And still... She remained, Compassionate, Merciful.

I read that frustration would never come,
But it did, in ways both petty and great,
And still... She remained, Serene, Unmoved.

I read that the movement of desire would subside,
But it arose, even in the midst of Fullness,
And still... She remained, Ecstatic, Rapturous.

I read that thinking would cease at last,
But it did not, only the "thinker" vanished,
And still... She remained, Silent, Still.

I read that fear would never again well up,
But it did, the "weather" of emotion continuing,
And still... She remained, Untouched, Unmoved.

All that I had taken myself to be, remained,
After The Divine Thief stole my self,
And still… I remained, no longer me.

So many things written in scripture,
Proved so terribly misconstrued,
After The Beloved Filled my Heart.

For all that had been before,
Though forever changed by Her Presence,
Remained thereafter…

Except for me.

MY HEART HAS BECOME EDEN

Oh Beloved, for this one, you broke the laws.
You took the scriptures from their holy place,
And hid them where I could not see,
Knowing their strictures would break my Heart.

Never have you whispered, "You must. You should".
Never have You held Your Heart from mine,
Until such time as I became "worthy" or accrued "merit".
You have Loved me, Always, simply because I Am.

I am your shattered cup, and yet…
You pour Yourself into me, until I overflow,
I am Your Lawless rebel, and yet…
You Free me, with every Heartbeat.

In the Garden of the Beloved

There was for me but one Hell,
That You would Love me "because",
That You would Love me "if",
That You would Love me "when".

There was for me but one Hell,
That You would require of me a ransom,
For the Fulfillment of my Heart's Desire,
The Kingdom of Heaven held hostage.

There is for me but one Heaven,
That as I and all creation am a part of You,
You have become a part of me,
And Shining Here, Illumine my Heart.

There is for me but one Heaven,
That Your Reveling in the Tavern of my Soul,
Has turned the water of my existence, to Wine,
Sipping which... more simply appears.

There is for me but one Heaven,
That the Healing and Benediction,
Flowing from Your Presence in this body,
Has raised the Lazarus of my Soul to New Life.

There is for me but one Heaven,
That the Rains of Grace, Showering,
Have transformed the desert that I was,
Into the Secret Garden that You Are.

My Heart has become Eden.

A DIVINE PUDDLE

When I and the world vanished, utterly,
And Heaven remained, as Nonexistent Existence,
I was not then a Christian, Jew, Muslim, Hindu, Buddhist,
Neither did God exist, or other than God.

Only after that Experience,
And the subsequent Presence in The Heart,
Of The Beloved's Perfume lingering,
Did I began looking here and there…

Wondering if I was alone In this Affair of The Heart.

I sought throughout the various religions,
Some reference to that Union of Nonexistent Existence,
And Her Sweet Perfume lingering, Intoxicating,
And found in each some Fragrance…

More so here, less so there.

But alas, I found also, always, inevitably,
The dogma and orthodoxy of each,
The varied descriptions of "reality",
Their assertive pronouncements of "truth"…

And found myself unable to linger.

I wondered, in heartfelt consideration,
If I must pour this Molten Mystery, unformed,
Into a framework of belief, a template of faith,
Forged by other Lovers, long ago…

Now held to by millions.

And I determined, in heartfelt consideration,
To leave my Experience Molten, Unformed,
A Divine Puddle, without center or periphery,
Uninterpreted, unexplained, remaining...

A Most Beautiful Mystery, a Puddle of Grace.

Now I dance through the villages of belief,
Like a madman, unfettered, a reveling child,
Splashing through the fountains of their Beauty,
Sidestepping, deftly, the muddy pools.

I cherish those aspects of every faith,
In which this Puddle finds Reflected,
In the Water of Love Unimaginable,
The Face of The Beautiful One.

I am now, in the sense that matters most to me,
A Christian, a Jew, a Muslim, a Hindu, a Buddhist,
"I am in Love", as Hafez declared,
"But with whom I do not know".

YES... SO?

A friend concluded, "All there is, is Consciousness",
And drew a flow chart to prove his assertion.

I said, "Yes... so"?

Another maintained, categorically, "There is one Self in all",
And elucidated his reasoning with great eloquence.

I said, "Yes… so"?

Yet another declared unequivocally, "Thou are That"
And propounded his logic with diamond-like clarity.

I said, "Yes… so"?

Still another pronounced, emphatically, "All is Emptiness",
There is no independent existence".

I sighed, "Yes… so"?

The Beloved whispered, "I Love you".
And my Soul cried out, wordlessly…

"Yes"!

OH MARINER OF LIFE

It was the play of desire and fear,
That drove my weary Heart Within;
Exhaustion, born of those dualities,
Endlessly pulling at my Soul.

Desire and fear, desire and fear,
Sailing desperately toward the one,
Struggling against the current of the other,
Losing strength with each breaking wave.

In the Garden of the Beloved

Perhaps you have heard the myths,
Of a Peace, imperturbable, impenetrable,
Where no currents move the weary Heart,
No waves disturb the troubled Mind.

"The Kingdom of Heaven is Within", he said.

Fearful at the risk of drowning,
But moved by desire for an end to strife,
Let slip the sails, oh Mariner of Life,
And Surrender your fate to the maelstrom.

Grace will respond, the promise is made,
To the wordless cry of your Heart,
And you will arrive, the promise is made,
At the Ineffable Sublimity of the Far Shore.

You will come, through Love and Longing,
To the vanishing of wind, water, and sky,
To the vanishing of the weary sailor,
Finding yourself Adrift, Nowhere, without your self.

No words can describe that placeless Place,
The Ocean You Are, without Beginning or End,
Where nothing yet is, and yet, everything is,
Without yet being.

Drowned, in the Fathomless Depths Within,
Fullness… Completion…. Ecstasy,
In the arms of The Beloved you left behind,
When first moved by desire and fear.

Then return to manifest existence,
Finding yourself still Adrift,
Nowhere… Everywhere…
Without your self.

KNOWING

What is this Exquisite Presence,
Shining Radiant in The Heart,
This Dissolution of dualities,
This Wellspring of Ecstasy,
This Fullness and Completion,
In which time, space, and myself,
Dissolve in Formless Rapture?

I don't know.

Is it not "Consciousness"?

I don't know.

Is it not "God"?

I don't know.

Is it not the "Soul"?

I don't know.

Is it not the "Atman"?

In the Garden of the Beloved

I don't know.

Is it not "Emptiness"?

I don't know.

I have only the Experience,
For which there are no words,
Around which no concepts are wrapped,
Of which there is no image,
Within which the knower,
Is rendered mindless.

From Attar:
"I know nothing.
I understand nothing.
I am unaware of myself.
I am in Love,
But with whom, I do not know".

From Rumi:
"I do not know who I am.
I am in astounded, lucid confusion".

Amen.

DROWN HERE

In my youth, starry-eyed, I wandered,
With countless others, starry-eyed,
The many stalls of the spiritual marketplace.

174

I found the cacophony more than I could bear,
So many voices proclaiming "truth",
That I could no longer decipher the meaning.

Too many arguments there, among "believers",
Too many assertions of right and wrong,
Too much contention among the orthodox.

And so it was that leaving the din and clamor,
The Way I found led away from those who "know",
Into the trackless wilderness of Unknowing,

How could I have imagined that it would be there,
In the Dark Night of Hopeless Despair,
That The Beautiful One would find me, and question.

"What treasure is left to you, now that all hope is lost,
Now that the Vultures have picked clean the bones,
Of logic and reason, faith, belief, and dogma"?

Searching to answer The Beloved, in the desolation within,
I found only the desiccated bones, crumbling to dust,
Of the many beliefs I had held to.

"Further, My Love, much further within" She urged,
"Back, behind, before... abandoning everything,
Even your cherished duality of 'I' and 'Thou'".

And so it was, with the wind of Her Love at my back,
I found, at last, in the deepest interiority of Being,
A Pool of Love, lost in ancient memory.

It was the taste of these Waters, I remembered,
That had first moved me to wander afar,
Away from my Soul, in search of The Ocean.

"Drown Here", She pointed, ushering,
"For the Water of your Soul is of the Ocean you seek,
In every drop, the Whole of the Ocean, Complete".

"In your very Essence, the Heart's Desire Fulfilled".

WHAT'S IN THIS TEA?

Strolling near Your garden,
The Fragrance took my Heart,
And my Soul began sobbing.

I knocked in Wonder at The Gate,
And opening ever so slightly,
Lest Heaven overwhelm me…

You held out this Cup.

What's in this Tea,
That its Fragrance alone,
Gives rise to Unbearable Longing?

Why is my Heart suddenly troubled,
With an Ancient Ache,
So Sublime?

How is it this pain of Longing,
Contains the very Sweetness,
Of that which is Longed for?

Not yet even sipping,
But in Fragrance alone abiding,
I cannot speak.... Intoxicated.

Tea to lip...
"I", so full in knowledge,
Am become a Doe-Eyed Fool.

Beloved, can you not tell me,
For surely you must know...
What's in this Tea?

"Surrender", She whispered,
"For this is the tea of Forgetfulness,
And Remembrance".

THE JEWEL WITHIN

Peace...
Not born of peaceful conditions,
Not born of peaceful circumstance,
But Inherent in the Essence of our Being.

Happiness...
Not born of happy circumstance,
Not born of happy conditions,
But Inherent in the Depths of our Soul.

Joy...
Not born of joyful conditions,
Not born of joyful circumstance,
But Inherent in our Deepest Interiority.

Dissolution...
Of the suffering self,
A Gift not born of merit or worthiness,
But the Love Child of Longing, Grace...

And the Quest for Heaven, within.

Ecstasy...
Not born of bodily sensation,
Not born of emotional elation,
But Inherent in the Presence of The Beloved.

All facets of The Jewel within,
Buried in The Depths of our Being,
But discoverable, oh Miner of Love,
When head and heart, Discernment and Longing...

Dig together.

THE PERFUME OF THE BELOVED

If the Perfume of The Beloved,
Were not sweet, seductive, and enticing,
Why would we care, for a moment,
To turn wandering Attention inward?

If She was without qualities,
If She was without attributes,
Why would we be drawn,
Why would a Lover care?

Why would we bother to venture within,
When the enticing enjoyments, without,
Are so readily available and alluring,
To our ever wandering Attention?

It is because She is So Very Beautiful,
Her Perfume so Irresistibly Intoxicating,
That we Journey into the depths of our Being,
To find Her there, as the Light of our Soul.

For when, arriving at the Heart of Being,
We Vanish into our Formless Essence,
It is Rapturous Ecstasy, beyond expression,
That is experienced in Pure Awareness…

At the end of all things, where everything begins.

THE FATHOMLESS DEPTHS OF THE HEART

What is revealed to the intellect,
Will never plumb the depths of Love,
For that Treasure lays beneath the waves,
Of cognition and "understanding",
In the Fathomless Depths of The Heart.

In the Garden of the Beloved

Reaching the end of thought's utility,
Consider with your Heart's Intuition,
What has been presented in the waves,
Of concept, theory, and dogma,
To the mind's limited capabilities.

Then sink ever more deeply, fathom by fathom,
The desperate mind holding its breath,
"Knower", "known", and "knowledge",
Dissolving in The Mysterium Tremendum,
Fathom by fathomless fathom.

Until, the mind Surrenders,
Unable to hold its breath any longer,
And swallows The Great Mystery,
Dying, at last, to the fruitless struggling,
To know, to grasp, to understand.

For no concepts can convey,
No images display,
Or words express,
What is revealed in that Final Gasp,
At the end of all dualities…

In the Fathomless Depths of The Heart.

THE KISS OF GRACE

I read one day…
That if I did not do thus,
And refrain from doing thus,
There would be no hope for me.

When I asked The Beloved of this,
She bound my hands, and Kissed my Heart.

I saw, the world over…
Brokenhearted souls struggling,
To perfect their imperfections,
Feeling it necessary to win Her Love.

When I asked The Beautiful One of this,
She covered my eyes, and Kissed my Heart.

I heard one day…
That from the multitudes of humanity,
Only a very few begin The Journey,
And that of these very few,
Only the most virtuous come to Her.

When I asked my Love of this,
She covered my ears, and Kissed my Heart.

In time, I fell into confusion and despair,
Having read, heard, and seen,
So many conflicting descriptions of "reality",
So many conflicting assertions of "truth".

 In the Garden of the Beloved

When I asked The Bestower of Grace of this,
She stole my mind, and Kissed my Heart.

When I told the orthodox of this Kiss,
They mocked my madness and delusion,
Chided my arrogance and conceit,
And forbade me burial in holy ground.

When I asked The Merciful One of this,
She buried me in Her Heart.

NOTIONS

I used to adhere to notions,
Notions held forth by this teaching or that,
As definitive descriptions of "reality" and "truth",
Presented with a particular form of "logic",
Argued, lawyerly, in often fierce debates,
Or… asked simply to be accepted on faith.

I used to adhere to the notion,
Of a "Ground of Being", a substratum of Existence,
Call it what you will; God, Jehovah, Allah,
Or Consciousness, so popular these days,
From which, within which, and as which,
All that is, arose, and vanished again into.

An Infinite Unmanifest Ocean, I imagined,
From which we, as manifest waves, arose and fell,
Waves of individuated Ocean, we were,
Having become lost in our individuation,
Forgetting our Essential Identity and Origin,
Suffering in identity as a wave, isolated and alone.

This… formless something,
This Ocean of Unmanifest Potentiality,
Though formless and unmanifest, was… Alive,
Not as a formless "thing" alive,
But as unmanifest Aliveness, prior to all "things",
From which all manifest "things" arose.

This… formless something,
Existed beyond the grasp of intellect,
Beyond the imaginings of heart,
And yet was Remembered in the Depths of Being,
As the longed for Heaven, Nirvana,
The Fulfillment of our Heart's Desire.

This… formless something,
Though beyond our grasp,
Enlivened our very grasping,
As if… as the manifest wave,
The Unmanifest Ocean,
Sought desperately to Remember itself.

I used to adhere to this notion.

But this notion, in time, was turned from,
As I changed stances, over time,
Taking refuge in notions born of other teachings,
Each providing words, images, and concepts,
That gave comfort to my heart's weary longing,
And kept my mind from the lunacy of Unknowing.

Over the many years of my life,
I have taken many stances, adhered to many notions,
But these days, near the end of things,
I hold the many notions mere… possibilities,
Neither declaring as true, nor decrying as false,
But seeing all as Villages of Refuge along The Way.

I used to adhere to a notion,
Of "what" it was that remained,
When I and the world vanished in Union,
And "what" it is that has lingered since,
Illumining the Experience of Being,
In Dissolution and Bliss.

But these days… these days…

These days, I see the Light in all notions,
For although this one may be true, or that one,
Or, from a certain perspective, all,
I take my stance with Farid Ud-DinAttar,
"*The sea will be the sea,*
Whatever the drop's philosophy".

These days, I see the difficulty in all notions,
For although this one may be true, or that one,
Or, from a certain perspective, all,
I take my stance with Hafez;
"The great religions are ships, and poets, the lifeboats.
Every sane person I know has jumped overboard'.

These days, in the Winter of my life,
I write from any stance, any notion,
Which presents itself most suitable,
In conveying, metaphorically,
That which has become, for me,
Beyond any stance or notion.

AT THE CROSSROADS OF HEART AND MIND

If you have not yet met The Beloved,
And wonder where She might be found…

Look within.

Let your Attention journey to The Tavern,
At the Crossroads of Heart and Mind.

And look for Her there,
With the eyes of your Soul.

If you wander off down the road of Mind,
You'll only reach a "conclusion".

In the Garden of the Beloved

If you wander off down the road of Heart,
You'll lose yourself in the imagined.

Journey to the Tavern of The Beloved,
At the Crossroads of Heart and Mind.

And look for Her there,
With the eyes of your Soul.

For She is your Essence,
Dancing in the Heart of your Being.

It is Her Great Joy to pour Grace,
Into a Cup held forth Empty.

But you must hold forth your Cup.

If you lose yourself in chatter there,
You will miss Her Silent arrival.

If you seek stature among those gathered,
You will see only yourself.

If you must have fellowship,
Commune with your empty Cup.

If you must yammer,
Speak to Her as if She is already found.

If you must think, reminisce,
Of that which was known, then forgotten.

If you must daydream, imagine,
The vanishing of all dualities.

Wait there, at the Tavern of The Beloved,
The Mind starved, the Heart besotted with Longing.

For if you have not yet met Her,
It is There that you will surely find Her.

Or rather, I should say,
It is there that She will surely find you…

At the crossroads of Heart and Mind.

SWOONING HEART AND BREATHLESS MIND

Far from the walled villages,
Of religion and philosophy,
Of belief and dogma…

Road vanished into path,
All certainty diminishing,
Ever less discernible…

Path vanished into hillside,
My satchel of words and concepts,
Dropped somewhere along the way…

In the Garden of the Beloved

Hillside vanished into Vastness,
"Where am I"?!
The Heart swoons in Rapture…

The Known vanished into Wonder,
"What am I"?!
The Mind collapses, unable to breathe…

Here I choose to dwell;
A choice in which I have to say,
I have had no say…

Carried, all along, as a willing hostage,
In the embrace of Swooning Heart,
And the arms of Breathless Mind.

IF WE ARE NOT MAD

Delivering bread, our beloved Hafez,
Saw the Beautiful Shakh-e Nabat,
And his heart, taken hostage,
Realized the Agony and Ecstasy,
Of worldly love.

Mad with Love and Longing,
In each delivery thereafter,
He sought whichever route,
However lengthy or out of the way,
Led him to the sight of her?

Mad with Love and Longing,
He did not hide away, pining,
But sought out every means,
Legitimate or contrived,
To glimpse her Beautiful Face.

Fulfilling a vigil to win her heart,
He beheld a Vision of Divine Splendor,
And turning from her visage in form,
Sought Her, thereafter, as The Beloved,
In the Kingdom of Heaven, within.

If we are not Mad for Love,
We will not seek Her with such passion,
Finding ways, legitimate or contrived,
To turn wandering Attention inward,
Chasing Her Perfume on the breeze.

For She is the Blossom of our Soul.

If we are not Mad for Love,
If She does not hold our Heart hostage,
Each breath labored in Longing,
Each heartbeat imbued with Yearning,
How… how can we hope to find Her?

For Love is the Secret Compass.

Her Heart, our warp and woof,
Her Love, the Essence of Our Being,
And only when Mad for Love,
Holding Her so very close,
Holding Ourself so very close…

Do Lover and Beloved Vanish in Ecstasy.

WHAT MATTERS NAME AND FORM?

I dare not speak of this Inner Presence,
This Radiant, Rapturous Sublimity,
This Warmth, this Richness,
This Fullness, Completion, and Bliss.

Oh, and I dare not say that She Resides,
In the Secret Garden of my Heart,
The Mystical Tavern of The Beloved,
In the Deepest Interiority of my Being.

For in Temple, Church, or Mosque,
The orthodox will assail me with "beliefs",
Of this Mystery they wrap in theologies,
Shining beyond such, in the Inner Sanctum.

With fingers pointing, I am "taught",
Prescribed what I must do,
Proscribed what I must not do,
"Reality" described, "Truth" asserted.

One will say, with certitude,
"This is the Holy Spirit"!

Another will declare, knowingly,
"This is Mother Shakti"!

Nondualists will curl their lips,
"This is mere phenomenality!"

Others will insist,
"This is the Touch of God".

And others will dismiss,
"You are simply delusional".

All that they hold forth is, to me,
Mere concept and conjecture,
Each possibly true, possibly,
Each possibly false, possibly.

I have no idea "what" She is,
This Beloved that inhabits my Heart,
This Exquisite Rapture,
Without center or periphery.

Perhaps She is the Holy Spirit,
For She both comforts the Heart,
And teaches the mind and Spirit,
Illumining the Whole of Being.

In the Garden of the Beloved

Perhaps She is Mother Shakti,
For although formless,
She moves within and as this form,
The Mover of this river's waters.

Perhaps She is the "Self",
The Ground of Being,
What I Am, before the World and I,
Before all of Creation arose.

Perhaps She is the Touch of God,
For Union was nothing short of Heaven,
And Her lingering Presence, here,
Healing and Benediction immeasurable.

And perhaps… perhaps…
I am simply delusional,
"Possessed", as Ramana felt, early on,
By a most Beneficent Demon.

What matters the name,
What matters the imagined form,
And dare I speak blasphemy…
What matters "Truth" or "Reality".

As our Beloved Attar has said,
Risking the wrath of the orthodox,
"The sea will be the sea,
Whatever the drop's philosophy".

MINDING WHAT HAPPENS

I read today…

"Don't mind what happens.
That is the essence of inner freedom.
Release attachment to outcomes,
And deep inside yourself,
You'll feel good, no matter what".

This seems to me poorly worded,
Or perhaps taken from a broader context,
In which greater exposition was provided,
So the Absolute and Relative perspectives,
Were not confused and muddled.

This is a problem with snippets.

For I mind what happens… immensely,
I mind with the Whole of my Being,
Even as I understand that all that occurs is,
From the Absolute perspective,
In the nature of things…

And as it is.

I mind the suffering of the world, terribly,
With the Whole of my Being,
Even as I understand that all that occurs is,
From the Absolute perspective,
In the nature of things…

And as it is.

I strive with all my Heart for an outcome;
For the end of suffering, everywhere, now, and forever,
Even as I understand that all that occurs is,
From the Absolute perspective,
In the nature of things…

And what will be, will be.

This "minding", this "caring",
This Heartfelt "desire for an outcome"…
None of it diminishes the Inner Radiance,
That Shines in the Heart of my Being,
Full, Complete, Inexpressibly Ecstatic.

I mind what happens… a lot.

in Union, in The Absolute,
There is no space, time, or self,
To care what happens, or wish for outcomes,
But only Timeless, Spaceless, Objectless,
Unalloyed Pure Being…

And what Is… Is.

But here, in this Dream of manifestation,
I pray and act with all my Heart for suffering's end,
Even as I understand that all that occurs is,
From the Absolute perspective,
In the nature of things…

And what will be, will be.

It is not a matter of "not caring",
But rather, a matter of accepting,
Of caring deeply, with all your Heart,
But having the Wisdom to understand,
That Heartfelt prayer and effort aside…

What will be… will be.

If I did not mind what happens,
And ache with all my Heart for suffering's end,
Then deep inside myself,
I would feel miserable,
No matter what.

In Love, I mind; in Wisdom, I accept.

WIND, PALMS, AND WHISPERED WORDS

I sat on the porch this morning,
Sipping coffee, puppy laying at my feet,
And as a sudden wind rustled the palm branches,
I heard, as clearly as ever I have heard,
Their soft, gentle whisper…

"Hello Friend".

Astonished, stilled in disbelief,
The mind pondering this dubious miracle,
Of wind, palms, and whispered greeting,
I spoke aloud, tenuously, embarrassed,
Feeling somewhat foolish…

"Hello"?

"No… not you", they whispered back,
"We greet the Blind, Deaf, Mute within,
Who Saw, Heard, and Spoke to us,
Before words and images arose,
Of "wind", "palms", and whispered greeting…

"Hello Friend".

And so I abandoned "myself",
The seer, the listener, the speaker,
And resting before the sound of inner voice,
Before the appearance of inner sight,
Before I and the world were born, I Heard…

"Hello Friend". and answered in Silence.

LOVE TURNED THE TIDE

I understand what it's like,
To turn attention inward,
And not be Greeted…

To hear only the chattering mind,
And be bound to its movements,
As the thinker…

To feel only the contraction,
Of the body, gross and subtle,
That ancient felt sense; dense, and separate…

To feel the hollowness of spirit,
The absence of Communion,
The emptiness and despair…

To fall in terrible defeat,
In the war of self-perfecting,
Striving in vain to become "worthy".

And I understand what it's like,
To turn attention inward,
And be Greeted by The Beloved…

For the chattering voice within,
To remain, but simply unheard,
No longer the focus of Heart and Mind…

To feel the Body Unlocatable,
And in its place, formless Presence,
Alive, Radiant, Palpable, Visceral…

To know the end of struggling,
The end of attaining, grasping, holding,
And to Rest in the Arms of Grace…

In the Garden of the Beloved

For the Manifest Form, gross and subtle,
To sink like a salt doll into the Depths,
Of the Ocean of the Formless Unmanifest.

What was it, then,
That turned the tide of Despair,
And brought me, thus, to the Far Shore?

Love was the enticement,
That lured The Beloved near,
To Embrace this Weary Heart.

Love was the Song of Grace,
That drowned out the chattering mind,
And liberated Soul from thinker.

Love was the Wine,
That Intoxicated the form, gross and subtle,
As She poured Her Heart into mine.

Love was the Matchmaker,
Who brought us together,
Moving me into the Light of Her Gaze.

Love was the Victor,
To Whom "I" Fell, Defeated,
In my struggle for perfection and "worthiness".

THIS NOTION OF ENDLESS HAPPINESS

This notion of unbroken "happiness",
Seems to me a terrible misguidance.
This, of course, is simply my view,
Not to be confused with "Truth".
Perhaps I've simply not yet come,
To that place of endlessly unbroken,
Peace, happiness, and joy.

But for me, "happiness" seems the wrong word,
And never the real intention, I suspect,
Of the many faiths, the many beliefs
The many philosophical systems.
I suspect, instead, that what is meant,
Is a Fullness and Richness of Heart,
In all circumstances and conditions.

My experience of the Divine Presence,
Is not a "happy" affair, or peaceful, or joyful,
But, rather, Ecstatic and Rapturous,
Containing "everything all at once",
And yet, from a different stance,
Containing nothing whatsoever,
Of the opposites of agony and ecstasy.

In the Garden of the Beloved

It is not of this world of joy and sorrow,
Peace and travail,
Happiness and sadness,
Or any of the myriad aspects,
That arise in our dualistic experience,
Pleasurable or unpleasant,
Here in this Dream of Heaven and Hell.

When an old Friend passed away,
I sat on my porch, sobbing inconsolably,
While with each breath, each heartbeat,
Breathing sorrow, beating sorrow,
My Heart, like an Ocean of Grace,
Rolled forth wave upon wave upon wave,
Of Her Rapturous Ecstasy.

Confounding? Yes.

When I see sorrow and weariness,
In the eyes of a stranger,
Or witness the suffering of this world,
I am not peaceful, happy, or joyful.
What word to use for this Presence that endures,
There, in the heartbreak of witnessing,
And the actions taken through Compassion.

Sublimity... in the midst of happiness or despair.

Her Presence is Rich and Warm,
As if I am being Loved, by no one I can see,
As if I am being Held, by no one I can see,
As if I am in Rapturous Union,
With a Lover, formless and unlocatable,
Whether I laugh, whether I cry,
No matter the "weather", inner or outer.

She is like the Blissful Sky,
From which, within which, as which,
The ever-changing weather of manifestation,
Moves in serenity or turbulence,
Like clouds appearing from nowhere,
Roiling for a time in delight or sorrow,
Then vanishing whence they came.

So when I hear teachers speak,
Of endless "peace, happiness, and joy",
My head tilts like a confused puppy,
And my brow crinkles, bemused.
How nice for them, if it is so.
Holding Her hand I am Dissolution and Bliss,
And when we Embrace…

Ecstasy, Unimaginable, Inexpressible.

These accompany me,
Through the ebb and flow of peace,
The coming and going of happiness,
The transient movements of joy,
Through the ever-changing weather,
Of existence as a manifest Being.

In the Garden of the Beloved

THE PATHLESS HEART OF ALL PATHS

How can I not be a Sufi,
How could they turn me away,
When the Beloved walks the pathways,
In the Secret Garden of my Heart?

How can I not be a Hindu,
How could they turn me away,
When the Atman Shines Radiant,
In the locus of my Being?

How can I not be a Christian,
How could they turn me away,
When the Holy Spirit,
Comforts and Teaches with every breath?

How can I not be a Buddhist,
How could they turn me away,
When Empty of independent form,
I exist as an Interdependent Arising?

Who would refuse this Drunken Vagabond,
Dancing at every temple,
Crying at every altar,
Taking the dust of every foot...

Beseeching every Lord...
Yet thankful in every breath,
For Grace already received...
From The Beloved who remains ever...

An Incomprehensible Mystery.

Wandering the Wilderness…
Where no villages of belief are found,
Along the Pathless Path,
Through which all Paths Wander.

How can I be troubled,
If the orthodox embrace or shun me,
When All is Fulfilled,
All is Fulfilled.

SUFFERING

When I speak of Union with The Beloved,
Of Her Abidance in one's Heart,
I do not, for a moment, mean to imply,
That we no longer suffer,
The ecstasies and agonies,
Of manifest existence.

Attar was slain by the Mongols,
As The Beautiful One watched.

Ramakrishna's throat deteriorated,
With The Beloved by his side.

Teresa of Avila gasped for breath,
Never abandoned by The Merciful One.

In the Garden of the Beloved

The disease in Ramana's arm took his body,
As he drowned in The Fountain of Grace.

St. Francis, as well, suffered greatly,
Beneath Brother Sun and Sister Moon.

And on, and on, and on.

This notion that all suffering will cease,
In the arms of The Beloved,
Seems, in my experience, misguided,
For body, mind, and emotions,
Continue their inevitable play,
In the ever changing "weather" of manifestation.

However "transcendent" in one sense,
We are, in another, here, and embodied,
Moving in the Dream of space and time,
In duality, conditionality, and causality,
In the ephemeral apparition,
Of birth, growth, maturation, decay, and death.

It is The Heart, rather, that is Healed,
The Soul, rather, that is Comforted,
The Spirit, rather, that is Blessed,
In our Deepest Interiority,
In the Heart's Secret Garden,
Intoxicated, in the Tavern of The Beloved.

It is there that She resides,
Through the tears of our outer sufferings,
Within the laughter of our outer joys
Through the vicissitudes of fate,
In the shock of our birth,
And the whisper of our last breath.

Though Joy and Sorrow ebb and flow,
Laughter and tears come and go,
Faith and belief stand strong or collapse,
It is Within that The Beloved Shines,
Within, that the Merciful One Comforts,
Within, that The Wellspring of Grace flows.

Even so… I breathe the prayer,
That if Her Presence in this Heart,
Grants but one wish,
It be that all Hearts Illumine, Within,
And, even against the Laws of Creation,
That none should suffer, without.

THE TRIBES OF KNOWING

There are many "tribes",
Scattered far and wide,
In the Infinite Vastness,
Of This Incomprehensible Mystery,
Without center or periphery.

In the Garden of the Beloved

Each tribe holds fast,
To their own unique traditions,
Their own unique interpretations,
Their own unique descriptions,
Of "reality" and "Truth".

Their Elders point to the Mystery,
Beyond the edge of their encampment,
And teach, with certainty and authority,
That it is thus, and thus, and thus,
And one should do thus, and thus, not thus.

We are born in and from The Wilderness,
In and from the Boundless Unknowable,
But unable to bear that Crushing Immensity,
Seek shelter and safe haven in "knowledge",
In encampments of "belief" and "faith".

And so the tribes of knowing are born.

I, too, have sheltered thus,
While Journeying this life,
Finding comfort and commiseration,
In interpretations and descriptions,
Of an Infinitude beyond word or concept.

The intellect took refuge for a time,
Until, in time, each time,
Knowledge and understanding,
However much a solace to the mind,
Proved unable to Fulfill the Heart's Desire.

At which time, in time, each time,
I took leave of this tribe or that,
And, offering gratitude and Blessing,
Walked naked, again, into the Wilderness,
Of astounded, lucid confusion.

And in that Wilderness without end,
Knowing nothing, understanding nothing,
Walking in Awe, breathing Wonder,
I Died of exposure…

To Love.

I HAVE FLED THE WALLED VILLAGES OF BELIEF

I have run from those who "know",
Who assert aggressively,
Speaking with certitude and authority,
The experience and interpretation,
Of those now long dead,
Regarding "Truth".

These Knowers have every right to speak,
And others, every right to listen,
And I, every right to turn away,
From the contempt and disdain,
In which they hold,
Those who do not share their belief.

In the Garden of the Beloved

There are many tribes in this Dream,
Taking refuge in walled villages of belief,
Of right and wrong, true and false,
Decrying in their temples,
The Untruth of others…
Marching forth to vanquish the infidel.

I have fled the violence of ideology,
Of belief, faith, and dogma,
To wander the Wilderness of Unknowing,
Traversing its Immeasurable Vastness,
Having burned for warmth along the way,
All notions of "Truth".

I have fled to the mountains of Mystery,
And there, watch from lonely heights,
The movements of their armies;
Brandishing concepts, beliefs, and faith,
Like swords and spears held aloft,
To impose the ""Truth" on others.

Here… in this Infinite Solitude,
This Boundless Immensity,
Like my Friend Attar, I find myself,
Knowing nothing, understanding nothing,
No longer aware of myself,
In Love, but with whom, I do not know.

With whom I do not know, and yet…
At the risk of building the smallest lean to,
Which, in time, might become a house,
And in time, become a walled village,
I cannot keep myself from whispering,
So tenuously, the word for my "God"…

Love.

LONGING REMAINS

Hell was wandering this Dream of Life,
Not Knowing the Touch of The Beloved.
Heaven was dying in Her arms.

Who is this "She"
Of whom I've written countless words?
I… don't… know.

She is the Ineffable Presence,
Here in this very Heart,
Of Fullness, Completion, and Bliss.

What is this "Bliss"
Of which I've written countless words?
I… don't… know.

It is inherent in… Remembering Heaven*,
The Fulfillment of Unbearable Yearning,
A cry so plaintive as to break the hardest heart.

In the Garden of the Beloved

What is this Longing,
And that which is Longed for,
Of which I've written countless words?

I... don't... know.

Only Longing Itself knows,
But cannot speak in words,
Of Heaven, so far... yet here, in this very Heart.

And so it is,
Though Longing is Fulfilled...
Longing remains.

So it is,
Though Heaven's Light Shines within...
Longing remains.

So it is,
Though the Beloved's touch is upon me...
Longing remains.

So it is that even with Love Fulfilled...
The Light of Heaven Shining in my Heart,
Her touch always upon me...

My Heart bends like a rose,
In twilight's darkening,
Toward the Sunlight of Her Face.

And like a lost puppy,
I whimper and whine,
Even as I'm being Held.

* Our Essence, by whatever name it might be called.

THE SALT DOLL'S JOURNEY

You've heard, salt doll,
Of the Ocean of Pure Being,
Of Heaven,
And you begin walking,
From the Desert of dualities,
In the direction your Friend has pointed.

As you draw nearer,
Even before seeing It,
You begin to feel Moisture in the air.
And it is so... very... intoxicating,
Especially to one so... very... parched,
From a life lived as a "person",
As... "someone".

If you stop walking now,
You will continue to enjoy the fleeting mist,
Ebbing and flowing, as mists do,
But will remain a person, an enjoyer.

And, suffering that pain of separation,
You will grasp desperately to hold,
What cannot be held;
The Fragrant mist,
Sweet with the taste of your Heart's Desire.
And you will live out your life still thirsting.

Keep walking, Dear Heart.

In time, you will come to the shore,
And standing there, become so Saturated,
With the Mist of Heaven,
That Sublimity drips from your hair.

But even there, drenched in Beauty.
"You" will remain,
And suffering, will grasp, white-knuckled,
To fill the Hole in your Heart.

Keep walking, Dear Heart.

The Mist you feel is "of" the Ocean,
Wetness to that water,
But should not be mistaken,
For Immersion in The Depths.

However Sublime "your" experience,
It will never satisfy "you",
Will never dissolve "you",
Will never quench the Ancient Longing,
As long as "You" remain.

Keep walking, Dear Heart.

Walk on, salt doll,
Until the ideas you hold of your self,
Until the ideas you hold of The Beloved,
Until all concepts, theories, and imaginings,
Sink into the Depths beyond all dualities.

Keep walking, Dear Heart.

Walk on, salt doll,
Into those Living Waters,
Where, drowning in Grace, Mercy, and Love,
Breathing in Fullness, Completion, and Bliss,
"you" die, at last, unto Life…

And only the Ocean, The Beautiful One, Abides.

THE FURTIVE GLANCE

This "remembering" of the Beloved…
It's a Gentle affair…

Soft and tender.

Not a grasping after, a groping,
Seeking to hold and keep…

For She cannot be "found".

In the Garden of the Beloved

Not something "done",
But rather, being "taken"…

Through Love and Surrender.

A movement, through Remembrance,
From the Beauty of the outer…

To the Sublimity of the Inner.

Not abrupt,
But a furtive, sidelong glance…

"My Love… are you Here"?

A movement of Affectionate Longing,
But without expectation…

For She dwells not in the future.

Less a "moving toward",
Than a "waiting for"…

Here… Now… Still… Quiet… Longing.

Perhaps, at first,
The subtle wafting of Her Perfume…

The Fragrance of Heaven.

Then… the Warmth of Her Presence,
As the Heart Illumines.

And then…
The Embrace…

In which Lover and Beloved
Vanish…

And the Heart's Desire is Fulfilled.

THE MYSTERY THAT SHE IS

Whatever words you can speak of Her,
Are no more than sounds,
Echoing through The Mystery that She is.

Whatever image you may hold of Her,
Is mere imagination,
Appearing within The Mystery that She is.

Whatever concepts the mind births,
Are mere apparitions,
Conceived within The Mystery that She is.

But… the Longing in your Heart,
That ache, more ancient than time,
That, my friend, is Real.

For it does not arise from you,
Being a Gift of Love, immeasurable,
Placed there by The Beloved Herself.

Unspoken.
Unseen.
Beyond conception.

A Perfume, lingering, of Unutterable Beauty,
A heartbreaking memory of Love known,
And then, tragically forgotten.

A Longing that will, in time,
Carry you beyond time,
Where word, image, and concept, cannot go.

A Longing that will Blossom within you,
Until The Mystery that She is,
Shines within, inseparable from…

The Mystery that you are.

BECAUSE I LOVED HER

There are those who are refined,
In thought, speech, and action.
I studied the lives of these great saints,
Perfected in virtue and "spiritual" qualities…

And found that I was not one of them.

There are those who set their mind,
And move in fierce determination.
I admired those with will and discipline,
Who struggle and strive so admirably…

But alas, neither was I one of those.

There are those of diamond-like intellect,
Able to discern and articulate profoundly.
I listened to countless discourses,
From those blessed with eloquence of mind…

And found that I was not one of them.

There are those who persevere,
Against the powerful tides of doubt.
I have known many in whose Hearts,
Faith and Hope are alive and shining…

But alas, I was not one of those.

And so, when She showered Grace,
Upon this least of Her lovers,
Drenching my Heart,
I assumed it was because…

I Loved Her.

When Her Love Overflowed,
In the Wellspring of my Heart,
Flooding the Whole of my Being,
I assumed it was because…

I Loved Her.

When Mercy Shone like a Sun,
Upon one so wounded and broken,
So lacking in the great virtues,
I assumed it was because…

I Loved Her.

When I was showered in Grace,
Drowned in the Ocean of Love,
And Blossomed in Mercy's Light,
I assumed it was because…

I Loved Her.

Only after these Benedictions did I find,
That the Love and Longing I had known,
Were never for a moment my own,
But Gifts from The Beloved.

The Beautiful One, who,
Before the world was birthed,
And the Light of our souls first glimmered,
Before ever we Loved Her…

Loved us.

And if it had not been so,
If Grace had not proven to be,
Without cause or condition,
Then surely, surely…

I would have cried myself to death.

THE DIVINE BREEZE

Stillness has a unique Beauty,
An unmoving Sublimity,
But my nature is such,
That I cherish, even more,
The rustling of leaves,
The gentle swaying of branches,
In the sudden arising of a Breeze…

The Unseen, moving the seen.

And so it is, in the world within,
Where, resting in the Serenity of Stillness,
My Heart leaps at the Unseen Touch,
Of Her movement through my Soul,
The senses Rustling in Ecstasy,
The Whole Being swaying in Delight,
For which there are no words.

Moved by the Unmoving,
The Unseen, moving the seen.

A STRAND OF HER HAIR

So few believe it possible,
That one's Heart can become Illumined,
With an Exquisite Presence,
Unlike any other in manifest existence.

In the Garden of the Beloved

That which the Sufis call The Beloved,
The Hindus, Ananda,
Christians, the Holy Spirit,
And nondualists, the Self.

I cannot fault their disbelief,
In a world in which the mystical,
Is so often proven charlatanry,
And dismissed as religious hysteria.

I cannot fault their disbelief,
For I, too, was a cynic,
A rational, empirical man,
Who, being without mystical experience...

Dismissed it all as delusion or madness.

Oh... what a shock to the mind,
When the impossible occurred,
And through inward turning,
I found myself in Heaven...

Vanished, yet Alive.

Oh... what a shock to the mind,
When the impossible occurred,
And upon returning from Heaven,
I found my Heart imbued thereafter...

Intoxicated with Heaven's Ecstasy.

But none should believe me,
If it is not their experience,
For lunatics abound,
In this madhouse of the spirit.

None should believe me,
Until, driven within,
They discover, empirically,
That they are a strand…

Of Her Beautiful Hair.

DROOLING MIND

It's most upsetting.

My roommate, the mind, was quite happy.
All was understood and codified,
And could be recited and explained,
With such diamond-like clarity,
To any and all who would listen.

And oh, how he loved to be listened to.

And oh… how he dearly loved reading,
Learning more, and more, and more,
Gaining greater and greater "knowledge",
Deeper and deeper "understanding",
Articulating ever more clearly…

Respected and admired.

In the Garden of the Beloved

And then… The Beloved came,
Her Beautiful Face, Captivating,
Plying him with the Wine of Dissolution.
I watched, helpless, as he became a Fool,
Neglecting everything, Intoxicated…

Dreamy-eyed, for Her.

I actually found him one day,
Where he had fallen by the roadside,
Head lying upon the curb,
Drooling concepts and theories,
Conjecture no longer of use.

Simply pathetic.

As I gathered him up to hide his shame,
He could only mutter, "Love, Love".,
Until he swooned, again… lost.
And all that he had learned of God,
Poured out of him, at last.

He'll never live this down.

We still live together,
But seldom speak anymore.
He wants only to sing of Her Beauty,
But the mindless fool can find no words,
And Dances, instead, mumbling…

"Love, Love, Love"!

IF YOU SEE THE BELOVED

If you see Her through the trees,
And run after, seeking to grasp and hold,
Making such a clamor…

She will vanish, fearful of "you".

But… if you see Her there,
And freeze… barely breathing…
Grateful simply for the sight of Her…

She will not see "you".

And if you persevere in Stillness,
Frozen… barely breathing…
Tearful simply at the sight of Her…

She may turn and see Your Heart.

And if you freeze… barely breathing…
Awash in Unbearable Love,
You will find… in time…

That She approaches, and touches your Heart.

Resting in Loving Stillness,
Dissolving in the Bliss of Her Touch,
You will find, in time…

That She walks beside You, ever near.

In the Garden of the Beloved

Surrendering your separate existence,
Dissolving ever more deeply…
Lover and Beloved will disappear…

Leaving only the wind in the trees,
Where once they danced,
In Sweet Flirtation…

The two having Vanished,
Beyond all dualities,
In Heaven.

HER ONE RESPONSE

No matter the question I ask of Her,
Spoken within, in the language of words,
She has only one response…

Dissolution and Bliss.

Dissolution of cognition,
Dissolution of the language of words,
The Vanishing of dualities,
In a Rapture beyond expression.

When, longing for relationship, I ask,
"Oh, but that I could speak with you"?
She has only one response…

Dissolution and Bliss.

Dissolution of the one who would speak,
Dissolution of the one who would listen,
The Vanishing of dualities,
In a wordless Rapture beyond expression.

When I ponder how exquisite it would be,
To see Her in form, and touch my Beloved,
She has only one response…

Dissolution and Bliss.

Dissolution of the one who would touch,
Dissolution of the one who would be touched,
The Vanishing of dualities,
In objectless Rapture beyond expression.

When the mind pleads for knowledge,
Of The Mystery Incomprehensible,
She has only one response…

Dissolution and Bliss.

Dissolution of knowledge,
Dissolution of ignorance,
The Vanishing of dualities,
In a mindless Rapture beyond expression.

 In the Garden of the Beloved

When the Heart seeks to Love,
And longs to be Loved,
She has only one response…

Dissolution and Bliss.

Dissolution of the Lover,
Dissolution of The Beloved,
The Vanishing of dualities,
In a Rapturous Love without object.

And still… each day… I sit,
And seek to know, and see, and love,
Until, in Her one response I Vanish…

In Dissolution and Bliss.

JOURNEY WITHOUT END

I eschew the implied finality,
And the exalted loftiness,
Of words like "enlightened" or "awakened".

For in my long Journey I have seen,
It unwise at best, and delusional at worst,
To ever plant a flag and declare the summit.

However transmuting the milestones come to,
At endless junctures along The Way,
There is no finality to Endless Enlightening.

In all my long years I have never found,
The mythical "Perfected" One,
However Powerful, Eloquent, or Beautiful.

Rather, it is the Imperfect that I cherish,
Who move in Honesty and Humility,
Illumined though imperfect, with Perfection...

On this Journey Without End.

ASTOUNDED LUCID CONFUSION

When Shams* stole Rumi's Heart,
The Scirroco* of The Unknowable,
Blew through the mosque of Rumi's mind,
Entwining, around, within, and through,
Until the knowledge that had accrued there,
Became tinder for The Fire of Experience...

And a Brilliant Scholar became a Brilliant Sufi.

Through the brightening of Love's Ember,
Was the framework of the known,
Made ever more brittle, ever more dry,
And ignited into Flame, at last,
Through a fateful encounter, unexpected
With The Sun of Love...

Alight in the Heart of his Friend.

Then roof and walls collapsed,
Words, pages, chapters, books consumed,
Revealing, in the ashes of the known,,
The Love that was in knowledge hidden,
Veiled in words, concealed in concepts,
And Rumi lived thereafter, as he wrote…

"In astounded, lucid confusion".

* Dry desert wind

* Rumi's murshid

ARE WE NOT INTIMATE?

No "appointment" can be made,
No formality engaged,
In turning to The Beautiful One,
Nearer than near…

For are we not Intimate?

Such propriety is taken by Her,
As an insult to the Intimacy of our Love,
An affront to its Unconditionality,
And I am left standing, counting beads…

For are we not Intimate?

Wondering what, why and how,
How to do "right", and not do "wrong",
How to approach again, "correctly",
I break Her Heart.

Whereas…

If I approach Her door staggering,
Drunk on the Remembrance of Love,
And stand there, forgetting to knock,
She opens… and rushes to me…

For are we not Intimate?

For us, there can be no preparation,
No "proper" setting of the stage,
In expectation, anticipation,
Of arriving, touching, holding.

For are we not Intimate?

She responds only and Always,
To Tender, Gentle Longing,
An affectionate turning Within,
In which instant She stands…

Not in a distant Heaven, but… Here.

In the Garden of the Beloved

Whether She is God,
Whether She is what "I Am",
Whether Transcendent or Immanent,
She remains an Unfathomable Mystery…

But oh… so Intimately so.

THEY TOLD ME

They told me She would not come near,
For as I was, I was profane,
But She took me, profane, into Her arms.

For profane though I was, I Loved Her.

They told me I must cleanse myself,
For Divinity cannot abide uncleanness,
But She pulled me into Her Perfect Embrace.

For filthy though I was, I Loved Her.

They told me I should not speak Her name,
For my tongue was defiled by worldly speech,
But She planted words, like flowers, in my mouth.

For defiled as I was, I Loved Her.

They told me I must do thus, and refrain from thus,
If ever I hoped to Know Her Embrace,
But She required nothing of me, but Longing.

For worldly as I was, I Loved Her.

They told me I must first quiet my mind,
In order to experience Her Silence,
But I heard Her Voice, amidst the din and clamor.

For cacophonous though I was, I Loved Her.

Some told me there was nothing to be done,
For I was always already "enlightened",
But there was *much* to be done, in the way of Longing.

And desirous as I was, I Loved Her.

Others told me there was much to be done,
In the way of perfecting, evolving, ripening,
But there proved *nothing* to be done, but Love.

For lazy though I was, I Loved Her.

I must simply be a madman,
To have burned the scriptures for warmth,
Along the Way to Her Secret Garden.

But it was She who lit the flame,
And irreverent as I am, She Loves me.

I must simply be a Drunken Fool,
To write, as I do, sipping Her Wine,
When the sober have spoken contrarily.

But She is the Cup Bearer,
And Drunk as I am, She Loves me.

In the Garden of the Beloved

The orthodox fought to keep Hafez's body,
From burial in holy ground,
And only a miracle dissuaded them.

For "unholy" as *they* saw him, *She* Loved him.

If no miracle accompanies my death,
Bury me as a Wretched Sinner,
But leave room in my grave...

For The Beautiful One,
The Merciful One,
The Compassionate One.

Leave room in my grave for Love.

A BAND OF MINSTRELS

Faintly, at the edge of memory,
I still myself, and turn within to hear.

What is this music, drawing near,
A song from ancient memory plucked?

A harmony of Space and Time,
The Formless here, with Form, entwined.

A Gossamer Dream in song,
Of Ecstasy, and Love's Longing.

Slowly coming into view,
A band of minstrels dancing through.

Through this Precious Dream of Life,
This Timeless Dance, in Time.

Woven…
Their many lives in mine.

Though countless players form the troupe,
I see but One Love drawing near.

It is Her eyes in theirs that Shine,
And Hers reflecting here, as mine.

She in Life's dance embraced…
Spinning both Dream, and Dreamer.

Her Heart in theirs, Shining,
And theirs in Hers, Abiding.

And together, sweet players,
We dance away the years,

And all too soon…
To Her, return…

Vanishing… whence we came.

WHAT IF

What if you knew little of the walled villages,
Of religion, belief, faith, and philosophy,
And then experienced, one day,
What seemed, when considered after the fact,
A loss of consciousness,
The vanishing of Everything from Awareness,
Including yourself as the one aware, and yet...

Awareness continued.

And what if the nature of that Awareness,
Pure and unsullied by space, time, and objects,
In which even you, the experiencer, had vanished,
Was so Ineffably Sublime that words did not exist,
To express its Ecstasy, its Rapture, its Perfection,
The Fulfillment of your Heart's Desire,
An Experience worthy of the phrase...

The Kingdom of Heaven, within.

And what if you found yourself, thereafter,
Imbued always with the touch of that Heaven,
Felt as a Radiance in the Locus of your Heart,
Sometimes the ambient background of experience,
Sometimes flooding the foreground, powerfully,
Ever available to the mind's Attention,
Ever available to the Heart's Remembrance...

A Wellspring, within, of Union's Ecstasy.

And what if you then entered the spiritual marketplace,
In search of someone, anyone, to explain the Mystery,
Wandering the rows of stalls, past the shouting sellers,
Each declaring the "Truth", and decrying the others,
Until your eyes and ears could bear no more,
And your Heart, bruised, pleaded with you to leave,
The pedantry, the arguments, the profaning of Love...

And return to the Inner Radiance.

The simple Experience, not yet corrupted by the mind,
Beyond knowledge and understanding,
Not poured into the mold of another's interpretation,
Not bound by prescription, proscription, and dogma,
Not requiring you to do this, and refrain from that,
Without cause, without condition, ever present,
A touch of Heaven ever Shining within...

Love, Unimaginable.

And what if, in time, that Presence in your Heart,
Like a Wellspring of Transmuting Love,
Diminished the terrible pain of your self,
Leaving intact all that you had taken yourself to be,
But stealing from your experience, the felt sense of "you",
That very felt sense that had vanished that fateful day,
So long ago in time, when time and all things Vanished…

And only The Great Mystery remained.

And what if, now free of the need for knowledge,
You returned to the spiritual marketplace,
Moved now only by Curiosity, Wonder, and Love,
And found yourself Dancing past the stalls,
Stealing this jewel from here, that jewel from there,
Until, your satchel full to overflowing,
You Thanked them all, and Rested again…

To the Inner Radiance.

And what if you then were moved by Delight,
To declare in poetic verse,
"Ah… this Most Beautiful Presence,
This Shining Radiance within,
This Exquisite Rapture,
This Fulfillment of all desire,
The Divine Thief that has stolen 'me'…

I will call it God,
I will call it Brahman,
I will call it The Beloved,
I will call it The Holy Spirit,
I will call it Emptiness,
I will call it The Inner Light,
I will call it The Unnameable…

I will call it Love".

And what if you were told,
To your surprise and amazement,
By some among the Friends you made,
That the ember in their Hearts,
Ignited, to their Delight and Inspiration,
In moments of Relationship with you,
Shining ever more Brightly, over time…

Until they found themselves, in time,
Imbued always with the touch of that Heaven,
Felt as a Radiance in the Locus of their Heart,
Sometimes the ambient background of experience,
Sometimes flooding the foreground, powerfully,
Ever available to their mind's Attention,
Ever available to their Heart's Remembrance…

I will call it… a reason to live.

In the Garden of the Beloved

And what if these Friends, now Illumined,
Were told, to their surprise and amazement,
By some among the Friends they had made,
That the ember in their Hearts,
Ignited, to their Delight and Inspiration,
In moments of Relationship with them,
Shining ever more Brightly, over time…

Until friends of friends found themselves, in time,
Imbued always with the touch of that Heaven,
Felt as a Radiance in the Locus of your Heart,
Sometimes the ambient background of experience,
Sometimes flooding the foreground, powerfully,
Ever available to their mind's Attention,
Ever available to their Heart's Remembrance?

I will call it… the Transmission of The Flame.

And what if you found, over the course of your long life,
No finality in the milestones come to along The Way,
No flag to be planted, no summit to proclaim,
And that however Profound the milestones reached,
More should not be made of them than should be made,
Each being merely a Tavern arrived at,
A Garden of Grace come to…

WHAT'S LEFT OF US

The day will surely come, if you Love,
When you're no longer able to feel,
Where The Beloved ends, within,
And what's left of you begins.

What's left of you will swirl,
Tumbling and turning,
Like the confused waves,
Where river meets Ocean.

Are you two, Lover and Beloved,
Or One, dreaming of two?
What's left of you,
Will be too Drunk to ask…

Having sipped The Beloved's Wine.

The Beloved is the Living Water,
Within which what's left of us,
Sinks, Dissolving, like salt doll.

The Beloved is the Air,
Within which what's left of us,
Flutters like a dry leaf.

The Beloved is the Earth,
Which will receive what's left of us,
When we fall.

In the Garden of the Beloved

The Beloved is the Fire,
Consuming what's left of us,
Ashes, clinging to Her feet.

The Beloved is The Comforter and Teacher,
The Giver of Roses, the Server of Wine.
The Wellspring of Grace.

Nearer than what's left of us,
Dearer than what's left of us,
Hoo!

Where does what's left of us,
Seek the Wellspring of Grace?
Within… ever more deeply, within.

And what is the Key to Union,
To Liberation and Illumination,
To the Dissolution of what's left of us?

Love, above all else.
For like a fruit ripening, in time,
You become what you Love.

Love Itself.

HOIST THE SAIL

Hoist the sail of Longing, even in the doldrums,
On the chance the Winds of Grace might come,
And carry you away to Heaven.

No sail… no sailing.

Go to The River and touch the Waters,
In the chance The Current might sweep you away,
And drown you in your Heart's Desire.

No walk to the river… no drowning.

Rest, and fool the frenetic mind,
Into falling headlong into Dissolution,
While The Heart falls Heartlong into Bliss.

No Rest… no Dissolution and Bliss.

Surrender, quit struggling, quit fighting,
And Collapse into the Aliveness you are,
Like a wave resolving into the Ocean.

No Surrender… no Resolution.

Cease your endless wandering, out there,
And Rest, Attentively, in Here,
Until the wanderer Vanishes into its Source.

No inward turning… no Heaven.

 In the Garden of the Beloved

Relax the contracted focus of Attention,
On this, that, and the other,
And take in Everything… All At Once.

No Inclusion… no Wholeness.

Feel yourself as the Field of Perception,
Within which, from which, as which,
All appears and vanishes.

No screen… no Movie.

Find a place, thing, or Friend,
In whose Presence you are effortlessly Taken,
And allow yourself to be Taken.

No allowing… no being Taken.

Cry out with your Whole Being…
To Life… to God… to the Great Mystery,
For Union, Benediction, and Liberation.

No Longing… sand for dinner.

THE SWORD OF BELIEF

Oh, what trouble we create,
When we give name and form,
To the nameless and formless.

And oh, what harm we do,
When we declare our "belief" as "Truth",
Decrying all others as "false"…

Forging a Sword of Ideology.

Whatever word we use to name,
However we interpret and describe,
We rend Heaven asunder…

The "Heaven" of Pure Being,
Where, in Formless Perfection,
Name and form never were…

Where concept, theory, and conjecture,
Never clouded the Sky, obscuring the Light…
Of Fullness, Completion, and Bliss.

Only the mind shouts this, not that,
While the Heart whispers…
Both, neither, Incomprehensible…

I… Am.

Ah… but look!
There!
Right there…

I, too, have created trouble!

It seems in the nature of things,
To name, describe, and declare,
Even if these are whispered in Love.

Only let us… in our naming,
In our describing,
In our declarations…

Be moved by Love, and do no harm.

PERFECTION AND IMPERFECTION

It was Love that drove me inward,
Or longing for it, I should say.
For I did not find it in the world,
Nor did I find it in myself,
For it is not love, but Love that I speak of.

An yet… somehow… I knew of it.

Even in my selfishness,
I had a sense of its Presence,
Of Causeless, Conditionless Love,
That Shone simply because,
It was its nature to do so.

A Love in which "I" did not exist.

Even as I sought to grasp and hold,
For my personal satisfaction,
It was there... somehow in the midst,
Perfection in the stew of imperfection,
Flavoring my selfish ends...

Seeking only the Benediction of all.

It was there, mixed up in what I Am,
Like one of many spices in a masala,
But for most of my life, in lesser measure,
Flavoring the experience of being,
Only ever so mildly...

Confounding the imperfect one.

When, one day, I vanished in that Love,
I returned not Perfected, Purified of myself,
But with myself imbued by Love,
Transmuted, more and more, by Love,
Subsumed, more and more, by Love...

Flavored, more and more, by Love.

And this is the proof of Grace,
That The Beloved, Perfect and Pure,
Dwells in this vessel, cracked and broken,
And Fills these imperfect seams,
As only Merciful Grace can do...

With Love, Causeless and Unconditional.

In the Garden of the Beloved

When I die, as I suspect I will, still broken,
Still shattered, and far from perfection,
It is Her Presence within my Heart,
Her Grace within the seams,
That will carry me Home…

To the Perfection that I Am.

To the Perfection that we all are.

I AND THOU

Beloved, am I simply making you up?
Are you just an "imaginary friend",
Born of immature emotionality…

Mocked by the "empirically-minded"?

After all, is it not true,
That I found You in all Your Glory,
When I turned within, and found Myself…

Before I and Thou ever were?

Am I not That Unfathomable Mystery,
Existing before manifestation ever was,
Before the world and "I" arose…

Before I and Thou?

What is this desire, this yearning,
To be in Relationship with You,
As if You are other than I Am…

As if I am other than You?

Why must I make a "Thou",
Out of the Incomprehensible,
Out of the Unfathomable…

That is what I Am?

It is because, Beloved,
Here, in this Dream of manifestation,
I am Lonely without You…

You are Lonely without You…

Even as Our heart beats Fullness,
Even as We breath Completion,
Even as We swim in Bliss.

It is because, Beloved,
Here, in this Dream of Duality,
Relative I misses Absolute Thou…

Even as my heart beats Fullness,
Even as I breathe Completion,
Even as I swim in Bliss…

Even as Lover and Beloved are One.

It is because, Beloved,
I have made a choice to taste Your Wine,
And savor Your Perfume…

Even as I Am Thou.

It is because, my Love,
When You Dance with Yourself,
As I and Thou…

You need someone to Hold You.

JUST ONE MYSTICAL POWER

Beloved, the scriptures caution us,
To avoid the dangerous trap,
Of mystical powers.

But please, Bestower of Grace,
Grant me just one power,
One Gift, not for myself…

To Ignite the Ember of Love,
In weary Hearts, drenched in despair,
Arriving at the door of this Tavern.

Take a piece of Your Heart,
A gentle whisper of Your Grace,
And place it in mine.

Though this vessel is deemed,
In the minds of the "religious",
Unworthy, unfit, unclean…

Let Your Perfection Shining,
In the midst of imperfection,
Be Proof to others "unworthy"…

Of Loves Unconditionality.

But I warn you, my Love,
If you Imbue me thus,
I will most surely misbehave…

Pouring Your Wine,
Into every cup held forth,
By those who notice its Fragrance…

And ask if Grace is real.

If only I can Gift every drop,
Before you catch and chide me
For spurning the Laws of Good and Evil…

Filling every Heart,
Everywhere,
Now… and Forever.

It is Grace that calls us,
Grace that moves us.

In the Garden of the Beloved

IF THERE IS MORE

If there is more,
Here, where the Path has vanished,
She will have to carry me to it,
For She has crept into my Heart,
And stolen the lack, the emptiness,
That moved me along The Way.

In its place, the Beloved Thief,
Left a piece of Her Heart in mine,
And I cannot move, Intoxicated,
With the Beautiful Perfume,
Of Her Fullness, Completion, and Bliss.

I read the other day of great danger,
In becoming hobbled at any juncture,
Along the Way to Heaven,
And could only smile at my misfortune,
The Beautiful Thief's most tragic Gift.

For what am I to do now?
How will I ever become "enlightened",
While I remain Drunk at Her Tavern,
Outside the door of which…
No Path is to be found?

How can I be Hungry,
When I am Full?
How can I be Thirsty,
When I Drown?
How can I care for attainment,
When I rest in the Arms,
Of Causeless Grace?

If there is more,
Here, where the Path has vanished
She will have to carry me to it,
Or bring it to me, through Grace,
For I am hobbled, faint,
Besotted in the Ecstasy,
Of Her Loving Embrace.

Pour me another, my Love,
Your Face is my Heaven.
And touching my Heart,
As you hand me the glass,
Let us toast the end of Suffering,
And the advent of that Love…
In which Lover and Beloved Vanish.

If there is more…

IN TEMPLE, CHURCH, AND MOSQUE

I began a Christian,
And for many years dwelt,
In the village of that faith.

In time, becoming a Buddhist,
I stood with a different stance,
But remained, in the Essence, a Christian.

For I did not discard the treasure,
I had gathered there.

And when I became a Hindu,
I remained, in the Essence,
A Christian and a Buddhist.

For I did not discard the treasures,
I had gathered there.

Now, fancying myself a Sufi,
I remain, in the Essence,
A Christian, a Buddhist, a Hindu…

A Lover of The Beloved.

I wandered this life,
In search of the Divine Presence,
And drank in each faith the Wine,
That made this Presence Illumine…

The church, temple, and mosque of my Heart.

The Beloved Holy Spirit,
The Beloved Emptiness,
The Beloved Atman,
The Beloved Friend…

The Beloved, by any name.

Now that She possesses my Heart,
I find Her Dancing and Singing,
Wherever She recognizes Herself,
In the world… in others…

In temple, church, and mosque.

BECAUSE

We begin, so sadly,
Seeking unconditional Love,
In the world of conditionality,
Here, there, everywhere,

Again… and again… and again.

Here, there, everywhere,
From this one, desired,
From that one, admired,
Seeking, but never finding…

Again… and again… and again.

In the Garden of the Beloved

On and on we struggle,
To become and remain desirable,
To gain and sustain stature,
In the eyes of those who love...

Because.

To receive affection,
To garner respect,
To gain power,
From those who love and admire...

Because.

Because they find us attractive,
Because they think us gifted,
Because of romantic mystique,
Countless reasons...

Because.

But through Grace we may find, within,
A Love not born of desire,
Shining unconditionally,
Even as we love...

Because.

And we may be Blessed to see,
This same Light Shining,
In the Hearts of those we love,
Through the movement of desire...

Because.

A Light, a Love uncaused,
Shining for no one, or anything,
Yet touching everyone and everything,
Illumining even that love born…

Because.

And at last we may come, through Grace,
To a most Blessed collapse,
Of seeking to create and sustain,
Of struggling to grasp and hold…

Because.

Falling headlong into The Heart,
The one who loved through desire,
And desired to be loved,
Becomes, at last…

Love Itself.

Illumining even that love which arises…

Because.

OVERBOARD

I broke the rudder some years ago,
When I fought too hard to steer.
And the sail at some point after,
Was torn from the mast,
By the storms of circumstance,
And sank into the depths.

I do no recall the dark night,
When the stars above, guiding my way,
And the landed horizon toward which I sailed,
Both vanished, leaving me directionless,
Adrift in the Unknowable,
With only a Heart full of Longing.

I cannot remember when I tossed the oars,
Into the fathomless depths,
And abandoned at last, all effortful striving,
To come quickly, oh, quickly, please,
To Journey's end, to Longing's Fulfillment,
And found myself...

Adrift.

I cannot recall that time of struggle,
Of sail, rudder, and oar,
Of starry night's guidance,
Or landed horizon beckoning,
I only remember... Collapsing,
Surrendering... at last, Falling...

Overboard, into The Beloved's arms.

Sinking into the Depths of Her Grace,
Breathing in Her Living Waters,
The Infinitude before space,
The Eternality before time,
And Existence as Life, Itself...
Before ever I became a thing alive.

What can a Drowned man do,
In the way of pointing,
For those who drift by, enquiring,
Directions to the Kingdom of Heaven,
To Fulfillment of the Heart's Desire...
Except to point... overboard... into the Depths...

Within.

IT IS

Q: Is the mirror separate from the images reflected on it?
A: Only in the mind of the beholder

Q: Is the beholder separate from that which is beheld?
A: Only in the mind of the beholder.

Q: Is the mind of the beholder separate from the beholder.
A: Only in the mind of the beholder.

Q: Is the mind of the beholder real?
A: As real as the beholder.

In the Garden of the Beloved

Q: Is the beholder really the Beholder?
A: It is.

Q: Is it not also the beheld?
A: It is.

Q: And what is its nature?
A: It Is.

WORDS... NOT YET WORDS

The Beloved awakened me last night,
Whispering in words… not yet words,
That which cannot be spoken.

Words like countless butterflies,
Eluding the mind's grasp…
Alighting in the Heart.

I've held them Here, for you,
In Love's gentle capture,
Words… not yet words,

So that when next we meet,
I might open my Heart,
Ands see them fluttering into yours.

IN HERE

Everyone's running around "out there".

Everyone wants to hear and "think about",
Everyone wants to read and consider,
Everyone wants to watch and contemplate,
Everyone wants to gather and be inspired.

Who wants to actually turn attention within…

And Discover the Hearer,
Make Known the Seer,
Reveal the myth of the Thinker,
Where neither self nor other exist?

Come friends!

Pull attention from its outward wandering!
Rouse yourselves… within,
And discover the Mystery of "what" you are,
Before "who" ever came to be…

Before "you" and the world appeared.

It's "in Here" dear heart… not "out there",
Here, within, before here and there ever were,
Before space ever was.

It's "in Here" my friend… not "when" or "if",
Now, within, before now and then ever were,
Before time ever was.

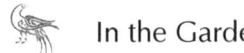

It's "in Here" oh vagabond… not "this or that",
You, within, before you and other ever were,
Before duality ever was.

Out there you hear about,
Out there you read about,
Out there you watch about,
Out there you gather and talk about…

In Here… you Are.

The Peace that endures,
Even as "peace" comes and goes,
The Bliss that Shines,
Even as "happiness" ebbs and flows…

Is… in Here.

For years, for decades, for a lifetime,
So many wander here and there, "out there",
Listening, seeing, talking,
Never stopping to turn within…

To the Kingdom of Heaven… in Here.

AN OLD COUPLE

It would seem I am no longer "spiritual",
No longer reading endless volumes,
No longer hearing again and again,
No longer chatting ceaselessly about,
No longer running here and there.

What has become of me?

It would seem I've quit the whole affair,
For like my breath, my heartbeat,
I no longer see Her as "spiritual",
For She has become, in these many years,
Inherent in the Experience of Existing…

Like wetness to water, heat to fire.

The mind seldom moves, anymore,
To the Temple of Knowledge,
To listen, starry-eyed, as She expounds,
Vanishing in the words,
Remaining as The Essence…

For Knowledge is Here.

The heart seldom journeys, anymore,
To the Garden of The Beloved,
To breathe Her Fragrance,
Vanishing as The Flower,
Remaining as The Flower…

For Love is Here.

In the Garden of the Beloved

The mind journeys to the Tavern,
The Heart to The Beloved's Garden,
Only when, sitting with a friend,
I hold the Loving Intention,
That Flame will ignite Ember…

Or in Celebration and Gratitude,
Of the Flame already Shining there,
In a Heart Radiant, Illumined,
With the Light of Heaven's Grace,
The Fulfillment of that Heart's Desire.

All fear has long since vanished,
Of Her coming and going,
All movement long since ceased,
Of grasping to hold and keep Her,
For She has proven Herself…

Ever… Here.

In the world of space,
No distance separates us,
For She Is… before here and there,
Ever came into existence.

In the world of time,
No duration separates us,
For She Is… before now and then,
Ever came into existence.

In the world of objects,
No duality separates us,
For She Is… before this and that,
Ever came into existence.

These days, like an old couple,
We don't yammer endlessly,
Words long since abandoned,
To express what cannot be spoken,
Fullness… Completion… Bliss…

In breath… in heartbeat… in existence.

Only occasionally,
For the sheer Joy of Expression,
As a Delight in the Dance of dualities,
Will I utter the words,
So Beautifully Inadequate…

I Love You.

THE WINE OF HER PRESENCE

I know nothing of an afterlife,
But am not concerned,
For I am so Intoxicated, Here, Now,
On the Wine of Her Presence,
That time has become,
Tomorrow has become,
A ghostly apparition.

In the Garden of the Beloved

The mind cannot move,
Its gazed fixed,
On the Lovely One.

I know nothing of God,
But am not concerned,
For I am so Intoxicated, Here, Now,
On the Wine of Her Presence,
That the hierarchy of flesh and spirit,
Human and God, profane and holy,
Has lost all meaning.

The Heart is breathless,
Still… but Shaking with the Ecstasy,
Of the Lovely One.

I know nothing of Heaven,
But am not concerned,
For I am so Intoxicated, Here, Now,
On the Wine of Her Presence,
That the mind is tongue-tied,
Muted in such considerations,
By the Beauty of Her Eyes.

If Heaven is Fullness,
Completion, and Bliss,
Then it is Here, Now.

I am not "perfected",
But am not concerned,
For I am so Intoxicated, Here, Now,
On the Wine of Her Presence,
Wounded and broken as I am,
That I can no longer wonder,
That Love is Causeless.

Before the terrible dualities,
Of perfection and imperfection,
She Is… I Am.

I know nothing of "enlightenment",
But I am not concerned,
For I am so Intoxicated, Here, Now,
On the Wine of Her Presence,
That the desire for "more" has vanished,
All movement "to and from" ceased,
As I Sink, Drowning, in… and as…

The Wine of Her Presence.

PERHAPS THEY ARE RIGHT

When I chat with my "ism" friends,
Buddhism, Hinduism, this ism, that ism,
They are quick to place my experience,
In the context of their beliefs.

In the Garden of the Beloved

They explain what has happened,
What it all means, and why,
Where I am on the Path,
Where I have to go…

And what I must do to get there.

They're certain and assured in all of this,
For the "truth" has been laid out,
And in their minds, unarguably,
By the founder of their ism…

And the "enlightened" who followed after.

Buddhism in all its many forms,
The vast ocean of Hindu philosophy,
The Abrahamic, book-based isms,
And contemporary "nonduality".

All certain and assertive,
Some speaking with the authority of "lineage",
Ancient, held in great reverence,
And in their minds…

"Truth", indisputable.

For Sankara said thus,
Buddha said thus,
Paul said thus,
Someone or other said thus.

And… perhaps they are right.

Seldom speaking from experience,
Most often my ism friends simply pour,
My experience into the mold,
Inherited from their ism.

Their intentions are kind,
For they find me sadly misdirected,
Bound in delusion and falsity,
In desperate need of guidance.

And... perhaps they are right.

I've no "idea" what happened that day,
When "I" and Creation Vanished,
When all dualities ceased, Absolutely,
Leaving nothing whatsoever,
Of knower and known,
Experience and experiencer,
Perceiver and perceived,
Subject and object,
But only...

Unalloyed Ecstasy,
Experienced by no one,
Before space,
Before time.

And I've truly no "idea" what this Radiance is,
This ever-present Sublimity that remained,
When the world and "I" reappeared,
Shining thereafter, in the Locus of The Heart...

In the Garden of the Beloved

A touch of duality's Dissolution,
A touch of the Ecstasy,
Inherent in that Dissolution,
As heat is to fire.

The world and "I" vanished,
Heaven remained,
The world and "I" reappeared,
And thereafter, a River flowed,
From Heaven into my Heart...

Into the experience of... Existing.

I've no "idea" at all "about" any of this,
No concepts, theories, or conjecture,
No assumptions made, or conclusions drawn,
Into which I can pour this Ineffable Sublimity.

And so, perhaps my ism friends are right.

For unlike me, they "know",
And are breathless to tell me,
The what, why, and wherefore,
From the "truth" as they "know" it.

And... perhaps they are right.

They place this Dissolution of dualities,
This Radiant, Blissful Presence,
In a "hierarchy" of "spiritual evolution",
From the "truth" as they "know" it.

And... perhaps they are right.

They explain, with certain authority,
How I am sadly in bondage,
Enamored of the "Bliss body",
Addicted to ephemeral experience.

And… perhaps they are right.

I do not know the "Self", they declare,
For there is no Ecstasy there,
No qualities or attributes of any kind,
In the "Absolute" they assert.

And… perhaps they are right.

They point to the use of words,
Such as "Lover" and "Beloved",
As sophomoric emotionality,
An immature desire for love and healing.

And… perhaps they are right.

It's all just kundalini, they say,
Nothing more than energy,
So much yogic hoo-hah,
To be dismissed as "unreal".

And… perhaps they are right.

They urge me to continue "further",
Striving to attain the "Ultimate",
Which they are happy to describe,
From the "truth" as they "know" it.

In the Garden of the Beloved

And... perhaps they are right.

In the words of each I find,
Varied teachings of "truth",
Varied descriptions of "reality",
Varied unarguable "absolutes".

All there is, is Consciousness, one declares,
All there is, is Emptiness, cries another,
All there is, is God, say others, still,
None of these are true, say the agnostics.

All so full of certainty,
So fierce when questioned,
So dogmatic, while claiming openness,
So righteous in seeking to help.

And... perhaps they are right.

But when Fullness, Completion, and Bliss,
Filled moment-to-moment Experience,
And the felt sense of ""self" vanished,
All movement stopped, to and from.

All seeking for "more" vanished,
All "grasping after" ceased,
And Bliss, Immovable, Impenetrable,
Filled, at last, this weary Heart.

In this Fullness, where am I to put "more",
In Completion, what is there to be added,
Intoxicated, the Heart's Desire Fulfilled…
Why would I seek a bottle.

But still… perhaps they are right.

TROUBLED

There are only a few lunatics,
For whom this "Great Matter",
Is more than a delightful fascination,
A reason to enjoy community,
A thrill born of occasional insight.

This is not an indictment,
As it's simply in the nature of things,
That most are satisfied just enough,
To have made peace with dissatisfaction,
Living and loving as best they can.

God Bless us all.

There are only a few lunatics,
Who, through no choice of their own,
Have minds consumed in Wonder,
Heart's Aching with Longing,
Who are, in a unique way…

Troubled.

It's a Blessing, not a curse,
To be thus consumed, thus distracted,
So that even amidst life's joys and sorrows,
One cannot escape the ever present Question,
Spoken wordlessly, in the Heart of Being?

What is this…
All of this…
This… being alive…
This experience of existing…
And… what am I?

A kind of Madness,
There in each breath and heartbeat,
Filling us, in the same instant,
With Unbearable Longing,
And Longing's Fulfillment.

A Longing born of that which is Longed for,
Containing, like a seed nurtured in The Heart,
The Fulfillment of the Heart's Desire,
Longing and Fulfillment, impossibly…
Present, both at once.

I find these fellow lunatics, occasionally,
And over tea we chat of The Great Mystery,
Of Her Inexpressible Beauty,
Words spoken in Love and Wonder,
Of that which cannot be spoken.

What a Blessing, that even now,
Through Grace, Unimaginable,
As Her Presence Fills my Heart,
I Ache with all my Being,
And Long for Her...

Troubled... Exquisitely.

BACK, BEHIND, BEFORE

You can sit for countless ages,
Listening to beautiful words,
About formless "You",
Within which "you" appear.

But if "you", in Solitude,
Do not turn attention within,
There is no hope that "you",
Will ever Know "You"...

As anything more than a concept.

It's not glamorous, sitting thus,
Alone... abandoning all that appears,
Abandoning the felt sense of "you",
And Feeling your way Back, Behind, Before...

To "You".

In the Garden of the Beloved

Back, Behind, Before...
To the Unlocatable Aliveness "You" are,
Before ever "you" or the world appeared,
And attention was drawn outward, fascinated.

There is no teacher, guru, murshid,
On the Journey to the Aliveness that "You" are,
Save the teacher, guru, murshid that "You" are,
Pulling "you" Back, Behind, Before...

Within.

You won't be rid of "you",
By hearing endlessly about "You",
By reading endlessly about "You",
Or talking endlessly about "You".

All of those must be abandoned,
Like baggage upon The Way,
Helpful in their way, early on,
But now heavy, burdensome, dragging.

"you", and the world must be let go,
As "you" Journey from the far frontiers,
Through ever-increasing Dissolution,
To "You", the Kingdom of Heaven...

Back, Behind, Before.

No sangha, tariqa, or community,
Can travel with "you", Pilgrim,
On this most Solitary of Journeys,
From "you" to "You"…

Back, Behind, Before.

But take heart, weary soul,
For if you persevere with earnestness,
"you" will Vanish, into the Ineffable Sublimity,
That arises as "you" dissolve…

In the Ocean that "You" are.

Have no fear, and be of Good Cheer,
For although "you" will cease,
"You" will remain…
Shining, Ecstatic…

Before even "You" ever were.

ONLY THE HEART MAY ENTER

I wandered in the "nondual" marketplace,
Among the countless "awakened",
Who feel that all there is, is Consciousness,
And simply understanding this,
Is all that is required.

In the Garden of the Beloved

While there is something to it,
On the face of things,
I found, upon lifting the facade,
An arid, cerebral affair,
Seeming to me, tragically misguided.

For though the mind lead me, truly,
To the Gates of Heaven,
There, reaching the end of its utility,
Having become blind, deaf, and mute,
It stepped aside, in Humility...

For only the Heart could enter there.

I fell, at that fatal juncture,
From Mind into Heart,
From concept into Feeling,
From understanding into Experience,
And Became...

What the Mind can only "think about".

My "enquiry" was driven by Love,
Not an academic investigation,
Searching to reach a "conclusion",
Based on irrefutable logic,
Presented with unarguable certainty.

For enquiry without longing,
Is a seed unwatered,
A seed unfertilized,
A seed blossoming colorless,
Without Fragrance or Flavor.

My desire was to Vanish… and Become.
To Vanish as the felt sense,
Of all I had come to feel myself as being,
And Become, in "my" Vanishing,
That which I had Loved and Longed for.

What was it I Loved and Longed for?

At the time, only a vague "remembrance",
Of something… Wonderful,
But long forgotten in Ancient Memory,
A sense of myself, not as myself…
And yet… My Self.

A Feeling, not a concept,
A felt sense of Heaven, within…
The Absolute Fulfillment
In the most Unimaginable sense,
Of the Heart's Desire.

I "Felt" my way to my Essential Self,
Before ever "I" and the world appeared.
I "Felt" my way to Heaven,
Before manifestation ever was,
And the Suffering inherent in dualities.

I came, through Mind, to that place,
Where I could not find myself,
But turning there, to the Heart,
Could Feel my Self... Alive,
As... Aliveness.

The thinking mind brought understanding,
Of the fact of my Formless Unlocatability,
But the Feeling Heart Experienced,
Beyond Understanding and Feeling,
What both Heart and Mind became...

What Is, before ever they were.

I PRAY

I pray, even though I don't believe in "God", as the religious do.

Praying just arose, over time, and took up residence in each breath and heartbeat.

Who do I pray to?

To no one, for I expect no answer. Nor do I pray for a result. And yet... I pray with Affection.

Why then do I pray?

Because I Love, and Prayer is simply its expression, like the Fragrance of a Flower, or the Warmth of the Sun.

My Baba spoke of "Divine Mother", though he said She was not, of course, a She, not an Indian woman in a sari; or a woman at all.

I lack the dear man's faith, and pray instead to The Great Mystery. Though thinking of it now... perhaps that is simply my name for Her, for my Beloved.

So now you know, when I speak of "Her", it is metaphor.

Metaphor, outwardly, for the Incomprehensible Mystery of Existence.

But lest that sound despairing, know that She is metaphor, inwardly, for a Radiant Presence of such Exquisite, Ineffable Sublimity, such Fullness, Completion, and Bliss, that any expression in words is folly.

It is this Presence that moves my Being in prayer, in every instant.

I pray for all of us; Healing, and Benediction.

For I have learned that it is not enough simply to be Healed, no longer be "sick", in bondage to all that we took our self to be.

That Healing, that Liberation, leaves a Serene Emptiness where "I" was formerly felt.

But this is not the Heart's Desire, to simply no longer be ill, however great a Blessing that may be.

No… we long for Benediction, for Fullness, Completion, and Bliss to pour into that Emptiness where we had suffered our self.

We long for the Sun of Bliss to Shine, not only within us, but to all, within all, in Blessing.

We long for the Wellspring of Grace to flood not only our Being, but to drown all who suffer its lack.

We long for Love, causeless and unconditional, to pour from the Cup we have received, into the Hearts of all.

We long for the Ecstasy of Formless Pure Being to Shine, impossibly, into manifest creation, drawing all… like a Divine Gravity… within… within…

Home.

There are no words in my prayer, and yet all the words in creation are there, Silently, in every breath and heartbeat.

Let all suffering cease, now… everywhere… and forever.

And if that prayer cannot be answered, if there is no Listener to answer, if it simply runs contrary to the "nature of things"…

I pray, none the less, that the Benediction I have received, from whence I do not know, will Shine in all, here in this Dream of Heaven and Hell, as they both suffer, inevitably… and Dance in Ecstasy.

God Bless everyone… everywhere.

RUMI'S MOMENT

Rumi turned spontaneously,
In a movement of Love.
Dancing with The Beloved,
In the Tavern of The Heart.

Beautiful, the falling leaves.
Dancing in Love's Delight,
With their unseen Lover,
The Wind.

Take no care of hands held thus,
Or feet moved thus,
Or movements made just thus,
For this dance is not such.

And Rumi's moment will be lost.

Find Her within,
Let Love turn your Heart,
And your Heart turn the world,
All and everything turned, truly…

By The Beautiful Choreographer.

In the Garden of the Beloved

THE DESERT

I could not turn back,
To the verdant forest,
Of the Great Teachings,
To take refuge there,
In those walled villages,
Of the known.

I could struggle no longer,
To know the unknowable,
To resolve all doubts,
Hoping, like the "enlightened",
To speak with certitude,
And powerful authority.

In that Desert, I fell down,
Brought low by fierce Honesty,
Strength and hope, exhausted,
All strategy abandoned,
All movement to and from,
Ceased...

Only then did I find,
Buried in my Heart... within,
What I had sought... without,
And Dying there, at last,
In that most unlikely of places,
The Seed of Grace...

Blossomed.

REMEMBER

If you don't Remember what you are,
Before the ever-changing weather,
Of psychology, emotion, and "you",
You'll... forget.

Remember to Remember.

If you don't extricate yourself,
From the powerful current,
Of "who" you take yourself to be,
You'll forget "what" you are.

Remember.

If you don't turn inward,
But are forever swept away,
By the waves of outer fascination,
You'll... forget.

Remember.

Remember... or be lost,
For in endless outward wandering,
We search like paupers, here and there,
Having forgotten the Treasure within.

Remember.

In the Garden of the Beloved

Inward, inward, within,
Before all that appears to you,
Before you, as you know yourself,
Weary vagabond, go There...

Remember.

It's not in talking ceaselessly "about",
Or reading countless words "about",
Or hearing yet more teachings "about",
Enough "about"!

Within! Within! Remember!

Fix yourself, fix the world,
Perfect the inherently imperfect,
Struggle and strive if you must,
But first... Remember...

The Kingdom of Heaven is within.

IN THE ANCIENT WAY

A single letter is written...
More letters form a word...
Words form sentences...
And sentences, paragraphs...

Paragraphs fill a page…
Page after page fill a chapter…
Chapter after chapter, a book…
And many books fill volumes.

Just so, "knowledge" is conveyed,
Concepts, theories, conjecture,
"About" the Mystery that we are,
And the nature of "reality"…

By those who "know" such things.

But in the Ancient Way,
Of the guru, the murshid,
No words need ever be spoken,
Or pages of scripture turned.

For in the most Ancient of Ways,
"Experience" itself is Offered,
Wordlessly… Heart to Heart,
Through Love's Mystical Alchemy.

No instruction need be given,
No prescriptions asserted,
No frowning proscriptions made,
Only, rather…

The Loving Evocation of Grace,
Two Drunkards at the Bar,
Two friends, glasses empty,
As The Beloved pours…

And Hearts overflow.

Just so, the Bottle is opened,
And The Wine poured Freely,
From one Empty Cup,
To another…

By She who is both Wine and Drunkard.

THE FRIEND

In the old days, my Baba said,
True teachers, gurus, murshids,
Did not sit "in front of" groups, elevated above,
But were simple people… simple…
Always sitting "across from" a simple friend.

They were fellow Lovers of The Beloved,
In whose Hearts Her Flame was alight,
And in relationship with whom,
The ember in one's own Heart would ignite,
And one would become, in time… "like them".

This is, after all, the point, is it not?

This was an intimate spiritual relationship,
Not seeing from a distance, seldom,
Over the heads of a crowd,
Not being "taught" in words and concepts,
But a Mystical Illumining of Grace…

Heart to Heart.

The guru, the murshid, the teacher,
Took tea with a friend, and chatted,
And together they bathed in the Presence,
That Illumined both their Hearts,
One aflame, the other igniting.

Things were said, questions asked, in this simplicity,
That would not be uttered in a crowd of strangers,
Revelations of the Heart's deepest Longing,
Questions utterable only in the Intimacy of Friendship,
And answers…

Born of a Heart Fulfilled.

It did not matter, my Baba said,
Whether the teacher, the guru, the murshid,
Was brilliant, of diamond-like mind,
Eloquent, and inspiring of speech,
Beautiful for the eyes to behold…

Or a drooling idiot.

All that was required, he said,
Was their Presence,
Which had become, over time,
Through Love, Longing, and inward turning,
Indistinguishable, inseparable from…

Her Timeless Presence.

In the Garden of the Beloved

Two simple Friends,
Two simple ones,
Two Lovers of The Beautiful Mystery,
Taking Tea, chatting, as only Friends can do;
Sipping… Sipping…

Vanishing in The Tea.

In this way, this Ancient Way, my Baba said,
The Flame in one, ignited the ember in the other,
And in time, when that ember burst into Flame,
Another teacher, guru, murshid was born,
A Simple friend, a Fellow Lover…

Of That for which "Love" is a wholly inadequate word.

Two things he oft' repeated:
"Slowly, slowly; She is doing everything".
And, more often even than that,
"Remain always, a simple man".

For the old days are now.

THE CROSSROADS

When the mind's capabilities are spent,
Having come to the end of their utility,
So few, it seems, take the turn,
At the crossroads of thought and Feeling…

And Journey on, to The Kingdom of Heaven.

Having come, through reasoned investigation,
To the truth of what they are not,
They do not, at that fateful juncture, take the turn,
From mind to Heart, concept to Experience...

Of what they Are.

This Grace at the Heart of Being,
Is not a reasoned "conclusion" come to,
Through mindful consideration,
Of logic and reason.

That which words and concepts seek to evoke,
Will die in the arid sands of the intellect,
A ghostly apparition wandering,
The wasteland of conceptuality...

For there is no Water there.

"I cannot find myself anywhere within",
I concluded, with a shock.
"But... I can Feel myself,
I can Feel my Self"!

And so I took the turn, Falling...

And, Dissolving into that Essential Feeling,
"I", and all of Creation Vanished,
In the Incomprehensible Mystery that Exists,
Before the world and I appeared...

And Heaven Is.

At that Crossroads, I took the turn,
When thought could reason no longer,
And Fell, Heartlong, into the Feeling of That,
From which the thinker, and all Creation arises…

And like a salt doll, Dissolved in that Ocean.

Had I planted a flag at the mind's conclusion,
And declared the summit attained,
I would have remained at the Crossroads,
Teaching "truth" as I knew it…

Selling water as Wine.

TEA IN THE WILDERNESS

If you've abandoned the walled villages,
Of belief, faith, and dogma,
And Wander, alone, in The Wilderness,
You will not encounter many others there,
Where those requiring "knowledge" fear to go.

There, where even a lean-to or rocky ledge,
Is too much shelter against the Great Mystery,
Where a single word says far too much,
Where the mouth is shut, but the eyes…
Like a child's, are wide open in Wonder.

There, when you chance upon a Wanderer,
Gazing within, Absorbed in their own Vastness,
Unaware of your awareness of them,
You do not intrude upon that Inner Temple,
But quietly set a trap for their Heart.

In a place close by, unseen,
You build a fire, and make Tea,
Waiting... ever so patiently to see,
If their Soul can sense the Aroma,
And turn to find, the Wilderness in you.

If they should turn, and come to Drink,
Nothing is spoken of belief, or faith,
For they, like you, have abandoned such,
And only the song of the birds is heard,
And the rustling of The Unknowable...

Through the leaves of your Souls.

I SPEAK TO HER

She does not wear a sari or hijab,
Nor is She of any race or ethnicity,
Espousing "beliefs" of any kind,
Neither is She a "she",
And yet...

I speak to Her.

In the Garden of the Beloved

The Beloved is metaphor,
For the Incomprehensible,
The Unnameable, beyond words,
And yet... resident in my Heart,
Here in this Dream of Existence.

An Unfathomable Presence,
Palpable, visceral, embodied,
Of Ineffable Sublimity,
Intoxicating Dissolution,
Fullness, Completion, and Bliss.

I speak to Her, as if She hears,
With every breath and heartbeat,
About the Great Mystery She is,
While "rational" friends deride me,
As a simple-minded "religionist".

But I, too, am a rational, empirical man,
Abnegating "belief" and faith,
Concepts, theories, and conjecture,
Wrapped around "spiritual" experience,
With no verifiable basis in "fact".

And yet... I speak to Her.

I suppose that makes me,
A rational, empirically-minded Fool,
For I've no "idea" to "what" I am speaking,
And no "belief" in "who",
For She remains to me a Great Mystery.

And yet… I speak to Her.

I speak in a wordless language,
For my very Existence is the Pray'er,
As it is the prayer Spoken,
And the Hearer, as well,
All at once.

Just so… I speak to Her.

I ask the impossible of Her,
In the face of all that I see,
All that rationality and empiricism reveal,
In the way of Love and Hate,
In the way of Beauty and Ugliness,
In the way of Hope and Despair,
In the way of Tenderness and Brutality,
In the way of Ecstasy and Agony,
In the ever-changing face of duality,
In the world… and within myself…

My Heart asks,
That all suffering cease,
Everywhere… now… and forever,
While the mind, rational and empirical,
Knows full well, that Creation is as it is.

And still… still, I speak to Her.

In the Garden of the Beloved

"I AM" BEFORE "I" AM

The Quest, as I knew it, was not "religious",
But outside of those walled confines.
In fact, I railed against The Great Traditions,
For telling us of Heaven and "enlightenment",
And then denying them to those of us,
Lacking in the requisite virtues.

For only the meritorious "attain",
Only the disciplined "transcend",
Only the "worthy" may enter,
Only those who "understand" will see,
Only those who "believe" are Blessed.

Rather, it was turning within, with all my Heart,
In search of Formless, Unmanifest "I",
Before manifest "I" and the world arose,
That took me to Heaven;
An inward turning which resulted,
In the Absolute Vanishing of all dualities...

Revealing I Am, without "I".

It was, in a sense, what I Am,
Before "I" and the world appear,
But again, not rightly "I Am", at all,
For there was no sense, at all,
Of a formless "something",
Aware only of ItSelf.

No thing at all alive, but only... Aliveness.

After the fact, I pondered,
As it seems all who have Vanished do,
About "what" it was that had remained,
At the End of all Creation,
And "what" it was that lingered here;
This touch of Heaven's Rapture…

In the Heart of "I", this Manifest Being.

But in all these years, I have found no words,
To describe the Indescribable Unmanifest,
The I Am, when "I" am not,
Or this Gift of Unimaginable Grace,
Here, in the Dream of manifestation,
My Companion, my Beloved… Myself?

It all remains, as do "I", a Great Mystery…
Experienced, but beyond grasping,
To Which I pray ceaselessly,
In a Voice without sound,
The Shining Heart,
Speaking to Itself.

WHY WRITE?

Why write?
To evoke that which is written of.
There is no other reason.

It is not to increase the writer's stature.

In the Garden of the Beloved

For if the writer were concerned over stature,
The words would not be worth reading,
Having flowed from a fouled pool.

It is for you that I write, not myself.
Because I love to see the Ember Brighten,
In the Heart of my friend.

I only share what we both possess,
As you so Beautifully share with me;
Both of us offering Love and Wonder,
One to the other.

We are two Lovers of the same Beloved,
Reveling in the Rich Delight,
Of the telling of our Life with Her,
And our ongoing Romance.

Not to vainly hear our voices speaking,
But to share Her Benediction in words,
Imbued, Mystically, with Her Presence.

Why write?

Love,
For Her,
And you.

THE MIND CANNOT ENTER HERE

The mind will lead you to the Gate
Of the Garden of The Beloved,
But there, in Humility,
Will stop and say…

"I have given you all I can,
Having brought you as far as I am able.
I cannot enter here, nor can you…
As long as you cling to me.

To enter Here, my friend,
You must fall into your Heart,
Surrendering knowledge and ignorance,
And Ache… with the Whole of your Being.

Only when that Key has opened the Lock,
Can you push open the Gate, and enter,
After which, Illumined with Grace,
You may return for me.

Then, the knowledge I have gained,
Will be transmuted into wordless Wisdom,
In which nothing whatsoever is known,
In Pure Intelligence.

And the Heart, Radiant with Love,
Will Shine within your very body,
Like a Beacon emanating,
The Light of Heaven.

And together, we two, Mind and Heart,
Will Vanish in Ecstatic Union,
Dancing…
In the arms of The Beloved".

THE OASIS

In the desert of separation,
So many journey in desperate thirst,
Drinking only concepts, dogmas, and "belief",
Never Falling from the arid Mind…

Into the Ocean of The Heart.

Desiccated by drought born of "religion",
Having wandered so long, so far from Living Waters,
They are no longer able to smell Moisture in the air,
And, journeying past the Wellspring of Grace…

Dismiss the Oasis as mirage.

Come! Come!
Drink! Drink!
Turn the water of knowledge,
Into the Wine of Love.

THE DUST OF HER FEET

It is She who will render you Humble,
For this is not a Gift,
You can give yourself.

The stone of selfhood will be crushed
Again, and again, and again,
Until only dust remains.

But in that Sweet Deconstructing,
There is no punishment exacted,
But only, ever, Love and Blessing.

And the dust that you become,
Fallen from Her Precious feet,
Will become, in turn, Benediction...

Taken upon the weary soles,
Of those who walk through you,
On their way to the Kingdom of Heaven.

HOW CAN THIS BE?

Holiness did not bring Her near,
But the Fragrance of Longing,
For I remain an imperfect masala,
Of body, mind, and Spirit.

And yet... as I am, She Abides within.

In the Garden of the Beloved

Some would have us believe,
That only the "worthy" can hope,
For the Beloved's Presence in their Heart,
For She will not dwell in an "unclean" temple.

But this is not my experience.

She does not judge, condemn, or punish
But is with me, as I am, to Teach and Guide,
Even as my density and recalcitrance,
Make each Lesson so very hard won.

But never does She abandon.

She does not curl Her lip in contempt,
Moving away, unable to bear my impurity,
Waiting at the gates of perfection, for my perfecting,
No… She is Here, in this muck and mire…

In the midst of what I am, as what I Am.

But… how can this be, the jurists ask,
When the flame of desire still burns,
Turning my eyes this way and that,
To a world of Beauty and delight?

And yet… as I am, She Fills this body with Bliss.

But… how can this be, the legalists assert,
When the mind still wonders endlessly,
Of Who, What, When, Where, Why,
Spinning in dizzying confusion.

And yet… it is She who Endows this Quest.

But… how can this be, the orthodox sigh,
When the sulfurous stench of fear,
Still visits this incautious spirit,
Bringing horrors, unimaginable?

And yet… as I am, She is my Guide in hell.

But… how can this be, the dogmatists argue,
When all that scripture declares prerequisite,
For proximity to Her Unimaginable Beauty,
Is so lacking in this tarnished brass?

And yet… as I am, She Embraces me.

It can only be, the mind surmises,
That however imperfect the vessel,
When the emptiness within it cries out,
The Merciful One cannot help but Fill it.

For as I am, the Beautiful One Fills my Heart.

It can only be, the mind concludes,
That the Law, in all of its power and authority,
Is, in the end, the prisoner of Grace,
And Yearning, the Victor in the Court of Love.

It can only be that the mind, as it is, is right.

NO RUDDER NEED BE HELD

No rudder need be held,
Nor oars be brought to bear,
No sails through effort raised aloft.

No charts laid out to view,
Nor compassed stars divined,
To guide along your Way.

No strategies employed,
Nor practiced skills perfected,
No disciplines willfully engaged.

Adrift upon The Mystery,
All direction lost in Wonder,
To The Far Shore you will come...

By Remembering what you Love.

REMEMBERING WHAT YOU LOVE

What is there to do,
But Remember what you Love,
And ache with all your Heart,
However distant Heaven may seem,
However much a fairytale and a Dream.

What is there to do,
But rest, with each breath and heartbeat,
In that U n b e a r a b l e Longing,
Which will not be consumed,
By the fires of doubt and despair.

For you did not choose to be stricken,
But simply found yourself afflicted,
With a Remembering beyond memory,
A Feeling beyond emotion.
A Knowing beyond knowledge…

As yet unKnown.

What else…
For when faith fails, Longing endures,
When belief crumbles, Longing endures.
When other's paths prove not our own,
Longing endures.

Longing… endures.

What…
But to Remember what you Love,
However She presents Herself,
Within the Secret Heart,
Of your own unique Longing.

You are not cursed, weary Friend!

For this Longing, Unbearable,
Is both Path and Guru,
For those of us so Blessed.
And Love…

The Key to the Gates of Heaven.

LIVING BY HEART

You become what you Love,
What you're fascinated with.
This was true, I found, as a musician,
When, through the sheer intensity of Love,
I learned to play…

"By ear".

And this proved to be true, I found,
In regard to The Beloved, where,
Through the sheer intensity of the Heart's Longing,
And the relentless focus of the mind's Fascination,
I came to my Heart's Desire, existing thereafter…

"By Heart".

I did not learn "spiritual theory",
Or practice long hours, or in fact at all,
Any science, technique, or methodology,
To come to what can only be described as,
Causeless, Conditionless Grace.…

For which… even the word "Love" is inadequate.

Unlike the world in which knowledge and skill,
Enhance our ability to express more beautifully,
The depth and breadth of our Inner Vision,
In matters of The Beloved… there is little use,
in the accumulation of knowledge or skill.

This, at least, is my experience.

The knowledge I have gained over time,
Of the vast and varied Paths to God,
Has only been of benefit, perhaps,
In understanding how others have interpreted,
The Unfathomable Mystery that Shines…

Uninterpreted, in my Heart.

For although there were times,
When I took refuge in this path or that,
I never "believed", much less had "faith" in,
The concepts, theories, and conjecture,
In which they all wrapped The Great Mystery…

The Great Unknowable.

I was drawn to each, for a time,
Not by their many doctrines or dogmas,
But by the Love I saw buried there,
Beneath all that demanded belief and faith,
Shining… still perceptible…

In the Garden of the Beloved

Through that dry, dead detritus.

But in the end, I returned, again and again,
To the Wilderness of Unknowing,
As a solitary Wanderer, but never alone,
In a Vastness so Great and Undefinable,
That the mind stops, and the Heart…

Shines.

For how do I describe, what do I call,
That Vanishing into Heaven that took me,
Into and as Incomprehensible Union?
And how do I describe, what do I call,
This Radiant Ecstasy that has shone, thereafter…

in the Wellspring of The Heart?

I use words from every tradition,
For in each there is such Great Beauty,
Though each, in their way, falls short,
And fails to express the Inexpressible,
This Unfathomable, Unknowable…

Mystery.

BLOWING ON THE EMBER

I only write of this Unfathomable Mystery,
This Radiant, Sublime Inner Radiance,
To bring it to Remembrance in the hearts
Of weary souls who have somehow Forgotten.

To blow upon that ember glimmering,
In the darkness of despair,
And pray, with all of my Heart,
That words, imbued, will ignite that ember.

If that ember is already alight and Shining,
Then I write to rouse the Wild Dancer within,
In Celebration of Love's Intoxicating Delight,
From words soaked in that Wine.

Oh, and here is the secret of Love I have found…
That Loving more, more Love arises,
And Blessing more, more Blessing's flow,
In an Endless River of Benediction…

Flowing not to, but from the Ocean of Grace.

Behind, within, these many words,
An Ache both Sorrowful and Beautiful,
For the Liberation from Suffering of weary Hearts,
And their Benediction, their Illumination with…

What word could I possibly use?

I'll use the word that always gets me in trouble,
The one so horribly taunted and abused,
But Understood by those in whom it Shines,
Even if only as a faint glimmer...

Love.

IT'S YOU

Come, dear friend,
Let us sit together, you and I,
Taking tea in Silence, not speaking,
"Of" or "about" this Great Mystery,
Of which the learned go on and on.

Let us abandon all concept and conjecture.

Between us, what is there to say,
When neither knows a thing,
Of anything, whatsoever?
What need have we of concepts,
Basking in the Immediacy of Experience?

Must we know the what, when, how,
The why and wherefore?
Need we be confident, assured,
Offering up with certitude and authority,
An answer to every question?

Do we really want to hear,
More words "about"…
More descriptions "of"?
Let us sit Quietly in this Fullness,
And Breathe Her Perfume.

Come, dear friend,
Let us sit together, and take tea,
In Silence, not speaking,
"Of" or "about" this Great Mystery,
Of which the learned go on and on.

Knowing nothing…
What is there to say?
But… we can Sip this Mystery,
And savor the Unbearable Beauty,
Of Divine Ignorance.

At the risk of knowing just one thing,
I will venture this much:
That this Beautiful Radiance…
It's You!
Naked, before being clothed in "you".

How uncomfortable,
To say even that much.
As if I know anything,
About anything,
Whatsoever.

Maybe, if I whisper softly…
So softly there is no sound….

"It's You!"...
Unclothed by "you",
When only…

"Something Wonderful" remains.

IF, WHEN, AFTER

If the Love I sought had been outside of me,
There would have been no hope of finding it,
For I never had the legs of an outward seeker.

If it had been bound to the prerequisites of scripture,
All would have been lost from the start,
For I enjoy so much that they say one should not.

If renunciation and discipline had been required,
I would have wandered, forever, the land of the Lost,
For the need to do and not do, always broke my Heart.

If the perfecting of practice and technique were essential,
I would have been expelled in the first trimester,
For I was, from birth, a Delinquent of Requirement.

If the perfection of the "person" had been necessary,
This libertine would never have entered the Gates of Heaven,
For I felt, from birth, a Love beyond all conditions.

If Love had not proven the very Essence of What I Am,
This "I" that wanders the dream of space and time
Would never have found its way Home.

If, when, after…
These are the shackles that bind the Hearts,
Of those seeking the Conditionless within Conditionality.

What Grace it was, that drove me Within,
Where Vanishing, The Beloved was revealed,
As Home, as Heaven, as my very Essence.

THE INNER SANCTUM

How I love to visit temples, mosques, and churches,
But only because when I see or enter them,
The Temple of my own Heart Illumines in recognition.

Not a recognition of beliefs or dogmas,
But of the Effulgent Mystery that each enshrines,
So often obscured by the detritus of "religion".

My "nondual" friends think me naive and foolish,
In need of emotional healing, or simply delusional,
Or I would surely not enter these monuments to duality.

But having Experienced formless, unmanifest Heaven,
And returned, my Heart thereafter Illumined,
I no longer discern where nonduality begins and ends…

In the Garden of the Beloved

For Formless, Unmanifest Heaven now Shines... Here.

The Radiant Presence within the Heart,
Is none other than the Light of Heaven, Immanent,
And it is This Great Mystery which Dances in recognition...

Recognition of temple, mosque, church, or cathedral,
Of the Light in the eyes of fellow Lovers,
Of the infinite manifestation of the unmanifest...

And my own... Sweet... Existence.

"Love is my Religion", as a Sufi poet declared,
And where it Shines, my Heart Illumines in recognition,
Recognition of Love here... Shining there.

All of Creation is surely a Temple,
As are edifices built with hands, sweat, and devotion,
But my own Heart, the Great Recognizer of these...

Is the Inner Sanctum.

THERE COMES A TIME

There comes a time,
When we become quite mad,
No longer able to function in the "secular",
Without it becoming, magically, "sacred",
Without our perception of everything... changing.

There comes a time, after the secular becomes sacred,
When the Great Mystery is no longer a mere curiosity,
Wondered about on Holy days,
In occasional discussions with friends,
Or engaged in during moments of "religious" observance.

There comes a time, after curiosity Blossoms,
When the Great Question impinges on awareness,
Upon each moment, each breath, each heartbeat,
Even while occupied in so-called "worldly" endeavors,
And demands our Heartfelt Consideration.

There comes a time, after Heartfelt Consideration,
When we are "taken", with no choice in the matter,
And Awareness, as we've known it all our life,
Becomes ever more Dissolute, ever more Intoxicated,
As this Great Consideration has its way with us.

There comes a time, after we are "taken",
When we come to peace with this Loving Intruder,
This Possession by Grace, by Dissolution and Bliss,
And somehow, though at first it seemed unlikely,
The mundane work of day-to-day is accomplished.

There comes a time, after day-to-day becomes Illumined,
That we no longer remember a time in our life,
When She was not Radiant within our Heart,
The soft, ambient background of all Experience,
Welling up in Greeting at the return of wandering Attention.

There comes a time, in time,
When we diminish, and She increases,
As we, like a salt doll immersed, again and again,
In the Ocean of Her Presence, the Waters of Her Grace,
Dissolve ever more, ever more deeply.

There comes a time, as we Diminish,
That Her Increase ignites the embers of Longing,
In the Hearts of those we meet along the way,
Wandering, as we do, in this Dream of manifestation,
Here, on the Frontiers of the Kingdom of Heaven.

And when that time comes, in time,
Our friends cannot mistake the vessel for the Presence within.
For while they may hold us in Affection and Gratitude,
Reverence and Adoration is for Her Alone…

As She dwells in each of us, and all of Creation.

SOMETHING SO BEAUTIFUL

You start out not believing,
That anything so Beautiful could really exist.
She seems a fairy tale, imagined by the religious,
By the simple-minded, wounded and damaged,
In desperate need of emotional healing,
Willing to believe in anything…

If it only alleviates their pain.

It seems incomprehensible, implausible,
To one so rational and empirically-minded,
That the experience of Heaven, within,
Is anything more than a hypnotic trance,
Born of fanatical deprivation and fantastical imagination,
Simply a psycho-physiological anomaly.

And who can blame you, given the lunacy of religion?

Then one day, oddly enough, seeking to die,
Not through physical harm, but through will alone,
You come to the wholly unexpected Experience of yourself,
As the absence of space, time, objects, and… yourself,
And yet, Alive, as… what word could you possibly use…
Heaven; not a place, but…

The Unalloyed Ecstasy of Pure Being.

And when space, time, objects, and you return,
You are left inextricably perplexed, for the rest of your life,
For in a sense, the absence of you, was You,
While in another, you were not, nor had you ever been,
For there was no time, past, future… or present,
And no space in which a you could exist or perceive.

And yet… You were.

In the Garden of the Beloved

"How can you remember an experience,
When 'you' were not present"? they ask.
You cannot explain.
And this troubles your mind,
For you are a rational, empirical man,
Having experienced, empirically, the rationally implausible.

And so you are ushered into the world of Divine Madness.

Ushered into madness even further by the fact,
Seen as lunacy by the mind, but Benediction by the Heart,
That you never completely return from... Heaven,
That within your Heart (why the Heart, you wonder),
Is an Ineffably Sublime Intoxication, a touch,
Not simply of peace, happiness, and joy...

But the Inexpressible Ecstasy you knew in Heaven.

She is ever there, awaiting the return of wandering Attention,
Waiting like The Beloved for your outer fascination to end,
And for Attention to return, at last, to Her Arms;
Her Perfume, always Intoxicating, both mind and Heart,
In moments both sacred, and "profane",
Awaiting to embrace you, into Dissolution and Bliss.

Your Heart has become the Gate, the Wellspring of Heaven,
Here in the Dream of space, time, and manifestation,
The Garden of The Beloved, Her Tavern, within.
To this Heart, no questions arise, no dilemma perturbs,
No desire arises to "know", or "understand", or articulate,
For All is Fulfilled...

All is Fulfilled.

In the mind… the temple of rationality and empiricism,
There the scholars, the academics within you debate,
What was that, that happened on the day of your Death?
What is this… this… Presence, as much a part of you, now,
As your breath, your heartbeat… alive now, within you,
As the very Aliveness that You Are?

But no answers come; no answers will ever come,
Only a chaos of concepts, theories, and conjecture,
As useless as pictures of Wine and Perfume,
And… this is just as well, for the mind, poor fellow,
Is far too Intoxicated, far too Dissolute,
To make any sense of anything at all.

You start out not believing,
That anything so Beautiful could really exist.
It seems incomprehensible, implausible.
To one so rational, so empirically-minded.
And then you die, yet Live,
Returning… Possessed by Love,
Still rational, and empirically-minded…

But still… still… "knowing" Nothing.

THE MERCHANT

A merchant came to the Tavern of the Beloved,
Selling reasons, causes, conditions, prerequisites;
Ways in which we Drunken Fools,
Intoxicated on the Beautiful Cupbearer's Wine,
Could become "worthy" of Her Love.

In the Garden of the Beloved

We at the bar could not hear him clearly,
Against the music, dance, and laughter,
Nor could we see him through the Smoke of Love
That filled the Tavern to the rafters,
And, inhaled, flowed through our Hearts.

But feeling mischievous, we cried "Fabulous!",
And hoisted our cups in toast, "Huzzah!"
Then standing, stumbling, brought him to the bar
Where... to our utter astonishment,
He refused the Wine She poured...

And began...

Listing conditions, circumstances, causes,
Logic to be followed, conclusions to be reached,
All of these and much more, stated as needful;
Requirements for "attainment"...
And... for each, the price to be paid.

As a Kindness... we bought every book he sold.
Then, embracing the poor fellow, sent him forth,
Into the Loveless night of worthy and unworthy,
With a Prayer and a Blessing,
That Grace might Shower upon him.

And through the course of the night's revelry,
Drowning ever more deeply in Her Eyes,
Ever more Intoxicated on the Perfume of Her Presence,
We burned the pages, book by book...

To light the Dance floor.

THE FALL OF A SPARROW

There are times when I fear,
I will surely cry myself to death,
For the suffering of the world,
For the fall of a sparrow.

But Her Presence like a Sun,
Shining within the Heart,
Keeps the Harbinger at bay,
And Illumines even Sorrow…

Even the fallen sparrow.

Sorrow and Ecstasy, at once?
Impossible.
Relative and Absolute, at once?
Incomprehensible.

The Mind collapses,
The Heart surrenders,
Manifest existence is Illumined…
And The Beloved Smiles.

FIRE ON THE SAVANNAH

For some, it takes a fire on the savannah,
To drive the lion of Attention within,
Returning in fearful flight…

To the Cave of the Heart.

For some, without those Flames,
Attention wanders creation endlessly,
Moved by outward fascination.

There are those requiring no such fire,
But such is not my nature,
Driven, as I was, by a Great Sorrow.

Fleeing that most Ancient of Pains,
I returned to that Place, within,
Where I rested without Fear...

And drank from Living Waters.

I thank that Fiery Blessing,
That chased me like a Fierce Friend,
Until, at last, it saw me safely sheltered...

In The Arms of The Beloved.

AH... MY LOVE

I could call this Beautiful, Sweet Presence the "Self",
For it is the Shining into form, of Formless Pure Being...

But I choose to say, "Ah... my Love".

I could call this Beautiful, Sweet Presence the "Holy Spirit",
For it is truly The Comforter and The Teacher...

But I choose to say, "Ah... my Own".

I could call this Beautiful, Sweet Presence "Divine Communion",
For it is Beatitude beyond all reckoning…

But I choose to say, "Ah… my Nearest".

I could call this Beautiful, Sweet Presence "God",
For it is Unfathomable, Incomprehensible…

But I choose to say, "Ah… my Dearest".

I could call this Beautiful, Sweet Presence "Divine Mother",
For it is the longed for Tender Embrace…

But I choose to say, "Ah… Love".

Only words… for that which cannot be spoken,
For the Shining into form of Formless Pure Being,
For The Comforter, The Teacher,
For Love, Causeless and Unconditional,
For the Fulfillment of the Heart's Desire...

For The Unfathomable Mystery.

Ah… Love.

A MOST BEAUTIFUL SORROW

There is a most Beautiful Sorrow.
How can I ever explain?

In the Garden of the Beloved

So Beautiful…
I would never dream to "transcend".

A Sorrow Illumined by that Bliss,
Which is beyond Joy and Sorrow.

So Beautiful…
I would never dream to "transcend".

Born of the BitterSweet Transience,
Of our existence in this ephemeral Dream.

So Beautiful, so Terrible, and yet…
I would never dream to transcend.

Lovers of the Absolute would leave this world,
And vanish in formless transcendence.

I have been to that Transcendent Heaven,
And returned, not transcendent, but…

Illumined with Love's Immanence.

Love for this Wondrous World,
Of Heaven, and of Hell.

So Beautiful… so Terrible…
I would never dream to transcend.

I have drowned in Her Formless Embrace,
And awakened again on the shores of duality…

Drenched in the Water of Her Radiance,
Here, in the land of Joy and Sorrow.

Her Wine Intoxicates every Heartbeat,
Here, in The Tavern of The Beloved.

Her Fragrance Blesses every breath,
Here, in the Secret Garden of my Heart.

Here, in the midst of a Beautiful Sorrow,
So Very Beautiful… so Very Terrible…

I would never dream to transcend.

BitterSweet tears of Ecstasy and Agony,
Are shed for this Beautiful, Terrible World…

I would never dream to transcend.

IMMANENCE

I never sought knowledge or understanding,
Concepts to be remembered and contemplated,
Brought to bear in times of inner difficulty,
When such "ideas" are so easily forgotten,
Swept away in emotion or physicality.

In the Garden of the Beloved

I never sought to reach a "conclusion",
Come to after consideration and contemplation,
Of propositions held forth by this path or that,
A "belief", born of accepting this or that description,
Of the nature of "Reality" or "Truth".

I sought a change in the very Experience of Being,
Simply... what it feels like to be Alive,
Not in transient "spiritual" moments, however profound,
But in continuous, moment-to-moment existence,
In the midst of endeavors, sacred or secular.

I sought Fullness, Completion, and Bliss,
A Benediction which did not come and go,
Ever available, even as Attention wandered,
Here and there in the world of "outer" experience,
Or when seized by emotion or physicality.

I sought a Benediction not held hostage,
By the vicissitudes of circumstance or conditionality,
By the qualities and attributes of mind and body,
Dependent neither on doing, nor refraining from doing,
A Benediction of Grace without Cause.

Not a transcendence of manifest creation,
But an Immanence, palpable and visceral,
A Presence here, in the Field of Experience,
Shining, untouched, unmoved, impenetrable,
Both within, and as, this Dream of Duality.

I sought the Experience, not the concept,
Of the timeless, spaceless, formless Sky,
Within which the ever changing weather,
Of manifest experience appears and vanishes,
Shining, Immanent… in this very Heart.

Among the countless Paths to be taken,
Paths of doing this, and refraining from that,
Paths of renunciation, will, and discipline,
Mine was the Path of Love and Surrender,
For I came to Her simply by Remembering…

What I Love.

GOD HAS NO NAME BUT LOVE

I cherish the company of the troubled,
Those who yearn, Heartbroken,
For One beyond envisioning.

The lunatic fringe, to the orthodox,
No longer sane, perhaps never so,
Distracted in the Madness of Love.

The clergy protested burying Hafez,
In the depths of hallowed ground,
Finding his poetry… profane.

No matter that they relented, in time,
For my Friend is buried now,
In the Hallowed Ground of My Heart.

So few there are, thus lunatic,
So few for whom She moves,
In every breath and heartbeat.

Only those Mad with Love,
Will abandon "belief",
And wander this Vast Unknowing,

Where Wisdom is Surrender,
And Treasure is of the Heart,
And Hafez, met upon the Way, sings…

"God has no name but Love".

ENDLESS ENLIGHTENING

Is one "enlightened"
If one has experienced the end of space, time, objects, and self,
And yet continued to exist as formless Pure Being?

Is one "enlightened"
If, upon returning from Heaven, one is Illumined with Bliss?

Is one "enlightened"
With the cessation of identification with the manifest form –
Body, mind, and the felt sense of personal identity?

Is one "enlightened"
When one feels one's self expanded as all that is?

Is one "enlightened"
When one feels one's Self to be that Great Mystery,
Within which, from which, as which, all that is, arises?

Is one "enlightened"
With the cessation of identification even as that Great Mystery,
Within which, from which, as which, all that is, arises?

Is one "enlightened"
When one feels one's self to be neither all that is,
Nor that Great Mystery within which,
From which, as which, all that is, arises?

Is one "enlightened"
With the advent of Fullness, Completion,
And the cessation of grasping?

Is one "enlightened"
When one's manifest form emanates Grace?

I would never use a word implying such lofty finality,
Or allow others to use it on my behalf.

For it seems folly at the least, and delusion at the worst,
To ever plant a flag, and declare the summit attained.

My experience in relationship to The Great Mystery,
Is one of...
Endless Enlightening.

In the Garden of the Beloved

I SAW YOU WALKING

I saw you walking from the world of sorrows,
Into the far frontiers of the Kingdom of Heaven,
And my Heart lit, my Spirit Brightened,
As the pain of separation began to leave your face…

And the sunrise of Bliss dawned within your weary Heart.

I saw you walking, in tears of Longing,
Ever deeper within the Great Mystery of your Being,
The Fragrance of The Beloved surrounding you,
Ever more deeply, until… two walked, not one…

Thou… and The Beloved.

She danced ahead of you, Singing,
"Come! Come! Follow, my own!"
"Love! Love! Follow, my own!"
And the Ancient Sorrow vanished.

You came at last, to the Realm of Grace,
And imbued with the Strength of Love,
Pushed open the Gates of Heaven,
And finding your way to the Inner Sanctum…

Lover and Beloved vanished in Ecstasy.

No longer could you hear the taunts,
Of those shouting from the far frontiers,
Decrying your foolish naivete,
Mocking what they could not understand;

That you had, by Love alone, found your way,
From Desolation, to the Inner Sanctum,
And, held there, in The Beloved's Embrace,
Died to yourself, returning as Life…

The Mind, Bathed in Wonder,
Your Heart Illumined with Bliss,
The Beloved, dwelling ever now Within…
Heaven, forever Shining…

In the Wellspring of your Heart.

DISCERNMENT AND LONGING

Discernment without Longing,
Is an arid, cerebral affair,
However Liberating in its way,
It remains, in the end…

A light without warmth.

Longing without Discernment,
Can see Passion adrift,
In a river of emotionality,
However sincere, unable to find…

The Ocean of Blissful Union.

The Fruit of Discernment and Longing,
Is Liberation, enslaved Ecstatically,
Emptiness, Full and overflowing,
The Ineffable Unmanifest Reality…

Sublimely Manifest.

And yet… if by a cruel twist of fate,
It was demanded one be chosen,
And the other set aside,
I would choose to remain…

A Fool in Love.

WHAT AM I?

I never enquired, "Who am I"?,
For I was quite familiar with "who",
The name, the image of the "person",
That… "felt sense", and all that it entailed.

In my enquiry, it was not the "who",
But the "what" that intrigued me,
As I wondered what I was,
Before ever I'd been told, or came to know…

All that I had come to take the "who" to be.

"What" was I, before ever I knew I was human,
Man or woman, fat or thin, stupid or smart,
Desirable or not, in any of countless ways,
Before the long history of "person building"…

And the relentless concern for stature.

And so I turned Attention Within,
No longer thinking "about",
No longer moving in concepts "of",
But enquiring with all my Heart, through Feeling…

In search of "what", before "who" ever was…

Unable to turn my eyes upon myself,
To see the seer Within,
I saw, instead, that "what" I was,
Could never be found by sight…

Or by any sense revealed.

Except…
Except…
Except…
Except…

I could… Feel… myself.

I could Feel myself…
Not a thing alive, but simply,
Formless… Unlocatable…
Aliveness.

In the Garden of the Beloved

And so I Rested in this Feeling of "I",
And as Resting deepened ever more,
The Fragrance of Bliss began to arise,
Barely perceptible at first, so soft…

Like Jasmine on a gentle breeze.

And in time, "I" vanished… and yet remained,
As the Pure Essence of Myself,
Before space, before time, before objects ever were,
Before ever I was, as the subject-perceiver…

Before all sensations and perceptions, save one…

For Experience remained… without an experiencer.
And for this there are no words adequate,
No concepts or metaphors sufficient,
No images or forms analogous…

Though the scriptures speak of it as…

Unalloyed Ecstasy.
The Kingdom of Heaven.
Divine Union.
The Self…

The Great Mystery.

When manifestation returned,
The Heart was Blessed thereafter,
With the answer to my quest,
The Bliss of Heaven Shining…

Into the Garden of The Beloved.

The mind, desperate to "know",
Remained then, and remains to this day,
Unable to comprehend or understand,
"What" it was that Is…

Before Creation appears.

"What" am I?
Formless… and Manifest,
Nothing… and Everything,
Nowhere… and Everywhere…

Lover… and Beloved.

"Where" am I?
In my Journey,
Into the Kingdom of Heaven,
I have yet to discover…

Where I begin and end.

THE HIGHWAY OF GRACE

All those years in auto shop,
Under the hood, covered in grease,
Working on that candyapple red beauty,
That one day… one day I would drive.

In the Garden of the Beloved

One day,
After I learned "about",
And learned "how to",
Then… maybe.

All those years of furrowed brow,
Studying the manuals.
Learning the "truth"
About driver and machine.

I cursed as I rapped my knuckles,
Struggling to understand,
What, why, and how,
How to think, how to act.

But neither Thought nor Action,
Ever prepared me for the open road.
The Way of the Heart, El Camino del Corazon.
Where one Feels one's way.

One day, sick of manuals and tools,
Of reading "about" and dreaming "of",
I threw the top down, petulant, fired Her up,
And headed off, down the Coast Highway.

I never graduated auto shop.
I have no license.
I don't know a goddamn thing…
But man…
I'm driving.

Engine humming,
Wind in my hair,
Sky above,
Road below…
And a smile that says way…

…Way more than just happy.

There are those well read, and gifted,
With explaining the unexplainable.
They will help you "understand",
If that is what you seek.

Myself… I am simply a madman behind the wheel.

For some it's time to leave the manuals,
You'll never "understand".
Time to drop the tools,
She'll never be "ready".

If you're such a delinquent,
Hop in!
There's something about that seat.
This is the Highway of Grace.

SPEAKING

The only benefit in speaking
About that which cannot be spoken of,
Is if the words spoken are Imbued,
With the Heart's Mystical Alchemy.

In the Garden of the Beloved

Words spoken thus, in Love and Longing,
Transmute the Experience of Being,
Enveloping speaker and spoken to,
In the Fragrance of The Beloved…

Which Fragrance, followed in Longing,
Guides Lovers ever more deeply,
Within the Kingdom of Heaven, until,
At last, through Love's Grace they arrive…

At the Fulfillment of all Longing.

In which case…

Speak.

WORDS

There are words…
And there are words.

Some words arise,
From the Wellspring of the Heart,

And speak in a thousand ways,
Of that which cannot be spoken.

Angels along the road to Heaven,
Lovingly pointing the way.

Through a Mystical Alchemy,
Beyond all reckoning,

They turn attention Within,
Guiding those who Listen with the Heart...

To the Fulfillment of all Longing.

POOF!

I read the other day,
"All that need be done is to 'notice'".
My Life Experience does not agree.

I can only say that for me,
It was not a matter simply of "noticing",
Of "Understanding", or of intellectual clarity.

I saw clearly, upon first investigation,
And thereafter, with Diamond-like Clarity,
That I do not exist as an object...

Although existing occurs... Existence... Is.

That "fact" was irrefutable.
I need only turn my wandering Attention,
Inward, in search of its Source.

There was no little man inside this head,
Seeing, hearing, touching, tasting...
Thinking... Living.

In the Garden of the Beloved

There was no object-perceiver-experiencer,
Anywhere to be found, within,
In the Formless Aliveness I found myself to be.

But this Apperception, this "noticing",
Did not, for so very many years,
Remove the "Felt" sense of "I"…

Within the Somatic aspect of Being.

"Knowing" full well that I was not an object,
I continued to "Feel" that I was,
The somatic contraction of "I", not yet released.

The remnants of the salt doll "I", not yet dissolved.

While the Mind reveled in Liberation,
And the Heart, Illumined, Danced in Bliss,
"I" remained in the Body, like a virus.

Until one day… Poof!

Why did that ancient somatic contraction,
That Felt Sense, vanish that day,
After so many long years?

I will only say, with fair certainty…

It was not merely the ripening of knowledge.
Not simply the product of "noticing",
For understanding alone had proven to be…

A debit card without a PIN.

And I will say, with fair certainty…

That in addition to the Fruition of Mind,
The PIN required, was found,
In the concurrent Blossoming of the Heart…

In the Love that first moved…
My weary Heart, into to ever deepening Longing,
My weary Mind, into ever deepening Unknowing.

And in time, through the Fruition and Blossoming,
Of both Heart and Mind,
The somatic remnants of the Salt Doll "I"…

Were carried to The Ocean by those two Rivers,
Where they became, as they had been,
Before the birth of creation…

Salt Water.

OUTSIDE THE WALLS

Mystical Experience, Divine Communion,
Is not confined to the many villages of religion,
Or to philosophical systems, however profound,
However revered their expounders.

In the Garden of the Beloved

For there are those who Wander,
Outside the walls of scripture and stricture,
In the Wilderness of Not Knowing,
Whose Hearts are, none the less…

Illumined with Grace.

Far from the village,
Road vanished into path,
Path vanished into hillside,
Hillside vanished into Vastness…

The Known vanished into Wonder.

For these Wilderness Wanderers,
There are no descriptions of reality,
No systems of belief or faith,
And the name of God is…

"Great Mystery".

And yet, like a Wellspring, their Hearts overflow,
Whenever they find, wherever they find,
In sources so-called "sacred" or "profane",
That which invokes Within…

The Presence of The Beloved.

Neither a She, nor a He,
Nor a concept of belief or faith,
Or in any way "Known" in word or image.
But Known, palpably, viscerally…

In the Heart's Direct Experience of Grace.

Here… within the Manifest Being,
Wherein Blossoms the Garden of The Beloved,
As the Ineffable, Intoxicating Sublimity,
The Inexpressible Ecstasy of…

The Great Mystery.

10,000 HAWKERS HAWKING

Today I wandered the spiritual marketplace,
And heard 10,000 hawkers hawking,
10,000 children teaching,
And 20 held forth as 100.

So many voices,
So full of authority,
Young and old,
Certain and assertive.

Each having planted a flag,
Declaring the summit attained,
Each teaching their "conclusions"
As "Truth".

I brought The Beloved with me,
But She could not bear the din,
And ran from that place,
Staring back from my Heart, sorrowfully.

I could not hear,
Amidst that terrible clamor,
Her gentle whisper,
"My Own, leave this place…

And follow Me… Home".

WITHOUT EXPECTATION

You don't have to know or understand,
What awaits you at the Tavern of The Beloved.
Such expectation will only keep you from tasting…

The Wine that you Are.

Whatever imaginings you may have,
Of that which is poured there,
Are merely concepts, theory, and conjecture…

Half-empty glasses of lukewarm water.

Abandon expectation, and simply… Drink.
Abandon the mind, and simply… Taste.
Abandon concept, theory, and conjecture…

And simply… Experience.

Go to The Tavern without expectation.
Where would that be?
Within!

Within?

Yes…
Where within and without never were,
And you Shine, before ever anything was.

Before?

Yes…
Where before and after never existed,
And you Shine, outside of time.

Outside?

Yes…
Where outside and inside have never been,
And you Shine, spaceless.

But… can I exist without space?
Can I exist without time?
Can I exist without being an object?

Yes… as You Are before ever "you" were.

Go to the Tavern of The Beloved,
And drink the Wine of your own Pure Being,
Until "you" Vanish in your Cup…

Until the seed of Longing becomes vine,
The vine births grape,
The grape is crushed into Wine,
The Wine poured into the Cup of the Heart…

And The Beloved drinks you all down.

When you are gone, all will be Clear,
For in the Absolute Vanishing,
Of the one who desired happiness…

So much more than Happiness will Shine.

THIS TEMPLE

When embodiment grows wearying,
As it sometimes does,
I fall into the Temple of my Heart,
Where You reside, my Beloved.

Not simply "within" nor invisible, this Temple.
For You have, in Your Magical way,
Made this Temple all that is, or ever was,
Timelessly Now, in this Spaceless Space.

Each day I walk in Your Loving Kindness,
Each day surrounded by You.
Each day held in tender Affection.
Ever with You, in You, as You, never apart.

Everywhere, like a Dream within a Dream,
My feet walk upon You, my eyes fill with You.
In rapture and sorrow, I breathe You.
For where, in Creation, are You not?

When embodiment grows wearying,
As it sometimes does,
I fall into the Temple of my Heart,
Where You reside, my Beloved…

As my own Pure Being.

A DANCE OF APPARITIONS

When She and I were in the dance of flirtation,
Before Her Embrace, and Lingering Perfume…

Even then I found, to my Great Delight,
That I could do no wrong,
In the stance I held in Loving Relationship,
Be it deemed "good" or "bad".

And now that She is the Gardener of my Soul,
Having taken up Residence in this Heart,
I find, still, to my Great Delight,
That I can do no wrong.

For She neither increases, nor diminishes,
Whichever stance I might take in Loving Her,
Each Way proving Beautiful and Fruitful,
However varied in their natures.

Standing here, I am Her Lover,
And She, my Beloved.

In the Garden of the Beloved

Standing here, I am Her Child,
And She, my Loving Mother.

Standing here, I am Her Friend,
And She, my Wise Counsel.

Standing here, I am Her adversary,
Enraged at the Divine Plan.

Standing here, I Vanish,
Into Her… as Her…

And standing here,
Both She and I had Disappear,
Leaving only that which Shines,
Before ever "we" existed.

And although some decry the possibility,
I find it to be so, again and again,
That in whatever state I find myself,
Deemed "good" or "bad" by the scriptures…

She is there, accompanying me.

What Love is this,
What Grace,
Unconditional,
Unimaginable.

Oh, wearying debaters of "truth",
Let all be Free to Celebrate their Love,
All stances being "true", in their way,
All… merely… a Dance of Apparitions.

The Illumination of the Heart,
Is not born of the Way in which we Love,
But through the Mystical Alchemy,
Of Love, Itself.

ABOUTISM

Forgive me if I stop here…
Where I cannot find "myself" as an object,
And have discovered, with a shock…

That "I" am just a feeling, a felt sense.

Let me just rest here awhile,
Reveling in this Exquisite Experience,
Before we go on to think "about" it all.

To come up with words like Consciousness,
Or Brahman,
Or Emptiness…

Or… whatever.

Words to describe what remains,
In this placeless place, where I find myself,
Not a thing alive, but only…

Aliveness Itself; the Experience of Existence.

In the Garden of the Beloved

Words to explain the unexplainable,
To speak of that which cannot be spoken of,
To describe this Great Mystery...

Within which all descriptions arise.

It's enough for me to simply sit here,
Drowning in Wonder, that "I" do not exist,
And yet... the Ineffable Bliss of Existence...

Is.

On second thought...
You know what?
You go on ahead.

I'll catch up with you later,
And you can tell me all that you've come up with,
In the way of concepts, theories, and conjecture "about"...

This Unfathomable Mystery.

Just please forgive me if I appear uninterested.
For in the Immediacy of Experience,
In this Fullness, Completion, and Bliss...

I've lost all interest in Aboutism.

A FAIRY TALE

Through all my wanderings in this world,
Through the lustfulness of youth,
And the ambition of middle age,
I held, among my other desires,
The desire for...

A fairy tale.

A Dream of Heaven, of Love unconditioned,
A Dream of Ecstasy, not of the body,
A Dream of Peace, beyond imagining,
A Dream in which inherent suffering,
Was no longer.

A fairy tale.

Born empirically minded, yet full of Longing,
I would have none of faith or belief,
In things unprovable, and likely imagined,
Of impossible dreams born of the suffering,
Of simply being incarnate.

Fairy tales.

And so one day, seeking an end to Suffering,
I turned within, to the Unbearable Longing,
For what I knew I must have been,
Before ever I learned a word,
Before ever I knew what "I" was.

In the Garden of the Beloved

A fairy tale.

So many words I had read,
So many teachings of so many paths,
So disheartening, all, in the course of time.
Of the "Truth" they held forth, and the Ways to it,
My weary Heart would have no more...

Of fairy tales.

Within... Within... Within...
Past words, concepts, and images,
Of myself and the world,
And all that the senses presented,
Presented to... what?

A fairy tale.

There, beyond within and without,
Through Unimaginable Grace,
"I" Vanished, and all creation with me,
And that which Is before all that arises,
Was what I was, without myself...

The fairy tale no longer.

The Love, Ecstasy, and Peace I sought... I was.
That dream of Sufferings end... I was.
My Heart's Desire... I was.
All of this... I was...
When I was not.

Heaven, found to be True.

This is not my tale of Grace alone,
But each of ours, who ache with Longing,
Along this Path of Love and Surrender,
Loving that... for which no words exist,
And which disheartening experience deems...

A fairy tale.

Within...
Within...
Within, Dear Heart...
To the Feeling of yourself,
Before the Feeling of your self...

The Heart's Desire... Fulfilled.

And when the world reappears,
The Light of Heaven, your Own Pure Light,
Will Shine as it Shines already,
Within your Longing Heart,
Into this world of ever-changing Duality...

This... fairy tale.

You will exist in Fullness,
In the world of Fullness and Emptiness,
You will exist in Bliss,
In the world of Ecstasy and Agony,
You will exist, a Sublime Formless Radiance...

A fairy tale come true.

PERSEVERE DEAR HEART

Your Loving Attention,
Is the SunLight of your Being,
Shining outward in delight and enjoyment,
Of this Wonder of Manifest Existence.

But turned Within, in Loving Quest,
This Light will evaporate,
The clouds of obscuration,
That veil Wonder, beyond Imagining.

Persevere, Dear Heart…
Don't despair or lose heart,
When nothing but gray sky greets you,
The density of embodied selfhood.

Persevere, Dear Heart…
Not in will, but in Love and Longing,
Of your Heart's True Desire,
For which, long ago, all hope vanished.

Persevere, Dear Heart…
And the Impossible Dream will be revealed,
As the Fullness, Completion, and Bliss,
Of your own Formless Being…

Your own Formless, Unlocatable… Aliveness.

Persevere, Dear Heart…
In Loving Surrender,
To the Feeling, not the thought,
Of the Vibration of Being that you are.

Persevere, Dear Heart…
And discover in your own experience,
That Heaven is no myth,
But the experience of your Innate Ecstasy.

Persevere, Dear Heart…
For your long forgotten Home,
Awaits the turning of your Attention,
There… just beyond the clouds.

CREAM, TWO SUGARS PLEASE

Within… Fullness, Completion, and Bliss,
Without… She prefers milk chocolate to dark.

Within… nothing can be added, nothing taken away,
Without… everything comes to Her, and goes.

Within… Unmoving, Ineffable Sublimity,
Without… She experiences ever changing manifestation.

Within… joy and sorrow have never been,
Without… She Shines, even in the midst of tears.

Within… time and space have never existed,
Without… She is born, grows old, and dies.

Within... within and without never were,
Without... within and without ever are.

Within... no preferences, propensities, proclivities,
Without... cream, two sugars, please.

Within... The Sun Shines,
Without... All is Illumined.

ALL THIS NONSENSE

Gautama experienced a transmutation,
In the nature of his Experience of Being,
And, responding to questions about it...

Gave birth to Buddhism.

But when Gautama died, in no time at all,
There arose debate and disagreement,
About this, that, and the other...

About "true" Buddhism...

And there arose, from one View, many.

So it seems, with all great teachings,
The Master's passing, and in no time at all,
Disagreement and debate...

And the arising, from one View, of many.

How vast and varied, expressions of "truth",
Each indicative of the utter futility,
Of describing the Indescribable…

Of capturing The Great Mystery in a jar.

All in the nature of things, it appears,
But oh, so very wearying,
Wearying enough to drive one…

Within.

Within… where long ago in distant lands,
In the experiences of those long dead,
All of this nonsense began…

Within.

Perhaps we, too, should venture There,
And enjoining both Heart and Mind,
In that Inward Journey…

Find out what all this nonsense is about.

CRY OUT

I was not a good little boy.

If there is a Divine Mother,
Her ankles are scarred,
With innumerable bite marks.

In the Garden of the Beloved

Not the brightest of Her children,
But full of Sincerity and Longing,
I alternated between sorrow and rage.

I confess, my path was strange;
Kicking, screaming, biting,
And holding my breath…

In the faint hope of gaining Her attention.

I wandered for many long years,
Through the confusion of "beliefs", and paths,
With each, falling ever more deeply into Despair.

I read of Heaven's Glory,
Of Nirvana's Inexpressible Sublimity,
Of "Enlightenment", and "awakening"…

But Longed only for Love.

I read of doing this and not doing that,
And the use of will and discipline,
In practice and renunciation.

All of which broke my Heart,
And none of which I ever pursued.
For I knew, somehow, that what I sought…

Was Causeless Grace.

Neither created in conditionality,
Nor sustained through effort,
Nor dependent...

On anything whatsoever.

Do not deride, you who struggle and strive,
Saying I make excuses for laziness,
And hide in a delusional dream...

For you simply do not understand.

How Unimaginable it was,
Given all I had read, heard, and seen,
That crying out one day in the Fullness of Heart...

"How could You be so cruel"?!...

She gave me... Everything.

Not a perfected personality,
Not a life free of suffering,
But Her Presence Always...

In my Heart... the Garden of The Beloved.

Be incorrigible!
Cry out! Scream and Bite!
Then fall Helpless at Her feet...

And never rise.

 In the Garden of the Beloved

If you are like this Prisoner of Love,
There will be no choice in the matter,
For even when Hope and Faith turn to dust…

Longing… will… endure.

This is the path I travelled,
And the Destination, Unlocatable,
In which I rest.

Unbearable Longing…

Unbearable Fulfillment.

IN THE IMMEDIACY OF EXPERIENCE

In the immediacy of Mystical Experience,
There is no interpreting,
Or seeking to understand…

No utterance of words at all.

Only after the fact do some,
Driven by the mind's compulsion,
Give name and form to the nameless and formless.

They may do so with loving intent,
Allowing the mind to revel and celebrate,
In the only way it knows.

But in time, as others take their words,
And seek to emulate their Subjective Experience,
All manner of divergence and debate arises…

And the Fragrance of The Beloved is lost,
The Light of Heaven dims,
And Love diminishes.

They become soldiers of "belief",
Having never known, themselves,
The Immediacy of Mystical Experience.

What to do?
For this seems simply in the nature of things,
Arising again and again, in every age.

Experience,
Interpretation,
Dogma.

I will leave off interpretation and dogma,
And rest in this Exquisite Experience of The Heart,
Emanating its Qualities and Attributes…

In a language spoken,
Before ever words were uttered,
And Heaven and Earth were torn asunder.

WHAT TO DO

What is there to be done?
If I grasp after Her, She flees.

If I do thus, and refrain from thus,
Her Love, Conditionless, is offended.

If I make a Goddess of Her,
She cries at the loss of our Intimacy.

If I move in concept of Her,
She wonders why I am eating dust.

I am Her brother, and She my sister.
If I do not tease Her, She feels unloved.

I am Her son, and She my mother.
To offer recompense for Her Love,
Would break Her Heart.

I am Her Lover, and She my Beloved.
She fills my Heart with a Rapture,
Born of Heaven's Ecstasy.

Where would I go to find Her,
When She Shines… Here?

What would I do to win her Love,
Which is without cause?

I cried one day,
With the Whole of my Being…

360

And She Came…

Both of us Vanishing in Heaven.
Which, thereafter, Shone in this Heart.

What to do?

Ache with the Whole of your Being,
Cry from the Depths of your Heart.

These, alas, are not "techniques",
Not "strategies" employed to an end.

These must be native to our Heart,
And carry us away, helpless…

As Prisoners of Love.

Among the infinite paths,
Mine was of Love and Surrender.

This is the only Way I know,
And all that I can speak of.

Sadly, I am not much use.

FALLING AWAKE

It's like falling asleep, but remaining awake.
Like dying, but remaining alive,
This Falling into our Self…

In the Garden of the Beloved

Letting go of Everything... Everything.

As in falling sleep,
This abandoning is a pleasure,
Anticipation of Sublime Oblivion...

Of Death Unto...Life.

Even so is our inward turning,
As we cease our outward wandering,
And Fall, Heartlong...

Into our Essence.

Not a practice mastered,
A discipline perfected,
But a movement of Attention...

From known, to Knower, to... Knowing.

Surrendering... Everything,
Including "enlightenment",
"Bondage"...

And all such hellish dualities.

Vanished, the Lover, yet... Alive,
As the Formless Mystery from which,
Lover and Beloved arise...

Both Dancing for a time,
Through this Play of Form,
Then Turning, at Heaven's behest...

To Embrace... and Vanish, yet again.

STILL WATERS

You'll never think your way out of thought,
But you can Feel, ever, ever more deeply,
That within which, to which, as which, thought arises,
Until, Feeling ever... ever... ever more deeply,
You Become that Formless... Unlocatable... Aliveness,
And thought, though ongoing, is simply... no longer... heard,
Attention having ceased its outward wandering,
Resting... at last... Dissolving... into... as...
The Still Waters of its Unmoving Source,
The Kingdom of Heaven...
Within.

LET HER POUR

If you're thinking of all you've read,
The many Paths to God,
Or realization of the Self,
All of those many fingers...

Pointing to Heaven...

In the Garden of the Beloved

Think until thinking does no good,
Until the tepid water of "knowledge",
Fails to satisfy the Heart's Desire,
For Divine Intoxication...

And the Thirst for Wine consumes you.

Then Feel...
Feel what it is,
That cannot be found by thought,
Cannot, therefore, be described...

But can, none the less, be Felt.

And along this Path of Feeling,
Never stop and declare, "This is it"!
Opening a stall in the spiritual marketplace,
And speaking with certitude and authority...

The Way, the "truth", and the Light.

Rather... wait...
Wait...
Until the one who would declare,
Vanishes, along with... Everything.

And only Heaven remains.

And when you and the world return,
Rest in the ever available Presence,
Of that Formless Radiance,
Shining from the Sun of your Heart...

Into your Manifest Experience.

Then… if you would do the world a favor,
Resist the temptation,
To pour the Inexpressible,
Into an existing mold…

Or a new one of your creation.

If you must speak of it,
Do so in Love and Compassion,
And, from a Vessel empty of yourself…

Let… Her… pour.

SOMETHING KNOWN, THEN FORGOTTEN

Longing is the remembrance,
More ancient than ancient,
Of something Known… then forgotten.

Forgotten, but alive within us,
As the Heart's Wordless Cry,
For something Known… then forgotten.

However hopeless we may be,
However faithless we become,
This Longing endures.

In the Garden of the Beloved

We may despair of religion,
But Longing endures,
For That which gave birth to all religions.

Longing for That which cannot be spoken,
Not that we cannot speak it,
But because... there simply are no words.

But... you Know it... don't you,
Reader of these failing words,
You Know, in your Sighing Heart...

That which was Known... then forgotten.

STANCES

How many stances can be taken,
In the face of this Unfathomable Mystery?

Standing here, I am the Lover,
And She, The Beloved.

Standing here, I am Her Child,
And She, my Loving Mother.

Standing here, I am Her Friend,
And She, my Wise Counsel.

Standing here, I Vanish,
Into and as Her.

Standing here,
Both Lover and Beloved Vanish...

Leaving only that,
Which Shines before Manifestation.

All stances... Beautiful and Fruitful,
When taken in Love,
Taken in Compassion,
Taken in Tenderheartedness,
Taken in Honesty and Humility,

And when taken,
In the Fullness of their Fruition...

For the Benediction of All.

Wearying debaters of "truth",
Gentle your Hearts.

For even if merely a Dance of Apparitions,
All Ways, taken in Love...

Are Beautiful and Fruitful.

TOSSING THE OARS

There are so many Ways.
As many ways as there are Lovers of God.

Some say to hoist the sail
And wait patiently
For the winds of Grace,
Making yourself "available".

Sometimes, it seems, there is little else one can do.

Others say that when the winds do come,
We must use the rudder to guide our way,
Following the tried and true charts
Of those who have gone before.

Traditions can hold precious jewels,
Amidst the mold, detritus, and dogma.

Still others say that when the winds of Grace arrive,
We must row like madmen,
As if our very life depended on it,
Using our feet, if need be, to steer a course.

Effort has its place… for some, for a time.

All good Ways, these,
For those suited to each by their natures.

I came by a different Way, not by choice,
Finding Home and Heart
Not in a destination, a knowing, a state,
But rather, drifting without course, into The Great Mystery.

Realizing, after ancient eons, that what I sought
Could never be "found", known or understood,
Could never be earned, or accrued through merit,
I quit sailing, and Drifted... Helpless... Surrendered.

I took down sail, unlatched rudder and oars,
And threw all into the Vastness.
Then, beyond despair,
I simply... Quit.

The last breath of hope whispered.

Loving myself, unenlightened.
Loving Life, as it is.
Liberated, at last, from Liberation and Bondage.
Defeated in my quest for enlightenment...

By Love.

"How can I help anyone"? I asked my Baba,
"When I don't know where I am,
How I got here,
Or where I'm heading"?

"Everyone seeks knowledge, teachings,
Certitude, and authority,
Not the teary, wide-eyed gaze of an Idiot,
Lost in Wonder".

"You've made me very happy", he laughed.
"For I would have you no other way.
If you 'knew' anything,
It would break my Heart".

"Don't worry.
You'll Drift into others
Lost in the Vastness,
Who, like yourself, knowing Nothing…

Have Surrendered to Love".

THE VERDANT HEART

Sooner or later, someone asks, "How"?
"How to come to all that you speak of"?
And the Friend answers…

"Love. How else"?

Not simply a salve, as some say,
For the emotionally wounded,
In need of healing.

Not a compassion born,
Of self-serving,
Perfection of virtue.

Not a strategy taken,
A stance deployed,
In search of Benediction.

But Defeat, Absolute and Certain,
From which ashes arise,
Victory…

In the Vanquishing of the Victor.

Understanding will not bring you here,
However diamond-like its clarity,
However impactful the seeing.

You begin where you are,
Loving, and desiring to be Loved,
But become, in the end…

Love Itself.

Be prepared to have your Heart Broken,
Not by anyone or anything,
But by Love Itself,

And for that Broken Vessel,
To be made Whole and Complete,
By the Breaker of Hearts…

And made Radiant with Grace.

But if you will not dare to Love,
Then Truly…
You will never "Suffer" this Rapture,

But will remain on the Frontiers of Heaven,
Wandering the desert of "knowledge",
In search of Water which can only be found…

In the Garden of the Beloved

In the Oasis of the Verdant Heart.

PRAYER, DISSOLUTION

Sometimes spontaneously,
Sometimes consciously turning within,
I am swept into Dissolution and Bliss,
And... pray.

To whom?
To what?

I've no idea.

But tears flow,
And my Heart breaks in Longing,
Even as, in that Divine Embrace,
All Longing is Fulfilled.

How shamelessly dualistic!

Sometimes spontaneously,
Sometimes in consciously turning within,
I am swept into Dissolution and Bliss,
And do not pray, but allow, instead,
The one who prays,
To Dissolve into Formless Pure Being.

What is that Formless Pure Being?
Where is this Formless Pure Being?

I've no idea.

But space, time, and objects Dissolve,
And I, the experiencer, with them,
Formless Pure Being remaining,
No longer a thing alive, but Life Itself.

How shamelessly nondual!

Dualistic relationship with The Beloved,
Or nondual Dissolution into Formless Pure Being,
Tasting Sugar,
Or Being Sugar…
Life is, in each instance…

Inexpressibly Sweet.

ALONE OUT HERE

I thought I was alone out here,
Out in the Wild.

How sweet to find you in this Vastness.
Are you mad, as well?

If not, you will be.
Free at last from "sanity".

So few leave the village of the Great Teachings,
And wander Here, Alone.

In the Garden of the Beloved

The few I've met have been driven by Life,
To push open the village gates, and abandon all knowledge.

What drove you to such desperation,
Taking those fearful steps into the Inconceivable?

There are no concepts here for one seeking knowledge.
Your teacher, The Unknowable, will remove all certitude.

And have no concern of arrogance and pride,
For those are not possible here, in the face of… This.

You will never understand this Vastness,
Write a book, and offer guided tours.

Such a din in the spiritual marketplace.
While here, butterfly wings are raucous.

I walked the Path of the Idiot to get here,
Burning scriptures for warmth, along the way.

And dying, at last,
Became All That I Sought.

Even while remaining, a simple man,
Imperfect, wounded, and broken as any.

SOMETHING WONDERFUL

Deep beneath the foundation of his Home,
Mullah Nasruddin discovered a hidden cellar
Filled to overflowing with…

"Something wonderful".

Amazed, he found,
That upon "drinking",
More simply appeared!

The intoxication was so deep, so sublime,
He feared friends would think him mad, And mentioned nothing
of the secret hoard.

Until one day a friend, a fellow Lover of "something wonderful",
Became intoxicated, simply from Nazruddin's breath.
And asked what he'd been drinking.

Soon, other Friends became drunk on Nazruddin's breath,
And all were shown the secret cellar, and invited,
To "drink" it all up.

But as soon as a drop was tasted,
More simply appeared!
And more… and more.

Some hoped for "benefit".
Some imagined a lofty "purpose",
Some sought to discern the why and wherefore.

In the Garden of the Beloved

But whether benefit was accrued,
Lofty purpose discerned,
Or why and wherefore ascertained,

All such things aside…

Whatever it was that was found,
Was simply…
"Something wonderful".

It is not Nasruddin's cellar alone, Dear One…

"What's that on your breath"?

IF YOU LOVE

If you Love being Alive,
Being Alive will Love you back.
This, at least, is my Experience,
And all that I may speak of.

Not Loving, necessarily,
The ever-changing content of Life,
But Loving the unchanging Essential,
The fact of Being Alive.

Such Love will not put an end,
To the ebb and flow of sorrow and joy,
But will touch the experience of each,
Will touch the experience of Life.

Untouched by all that arises,
But Touching all that arises,
Love born of Loving...
And being Loved by...

The Mystery of Life that we are.

THE WILDERNESS OF WONDER

When I found myself without belief,
I Surrendered to knowing Nothing,
And learned to Love the Wilderness,
Though the mind continued to Wonder endlessly.

And when the mind could no longer bear,
The Crushing Immensity of Not Knowing,
I was moved by Compassion for it,
And sought a path of Wisdom.

But I found myself unable to live,
In villages laid out this way and that,
Walled about with "knowledge" of the Unknowable...

And walked again into the Wilderness.

When I found myself without faith,
I Surrendered to being Adrift,
In an Ocean of Solitude,
And learned to Love the Rudderless Way.

In the Garden of the Beloved

And when the Heart could not bear,
The Depth and Breadth of that Solitude,
I was moved by Compassion for it,
And sought a path with Heart.

But I found myself unable to live,
In villages laid out this way and that,
Walled about with "devotion" as each defined it…

And walked again into the Wilderness.

Heart and mind have Surrendered,
To this Wilderness Life,
To Not Knowing,
To Love Shining without object.

When the mind cannot bear,
The Crushing Immensity of Not Knowing,
It no longer twists and turns as one obsessed,
But gasps, Dissolute, in Wonder.

When the Heart cannot bear,
The Depth and Breadth of Solitude,
It no longer seeks another,
But falling into itself… gasps in Ecstasy.

MERCY

I cried out for Love,
But received, instead, my Heart's Desire

So much more, than the word Love,
Could ever hope to contain.

I would call it... Benediction,
Blessing, beyond measure, ever present.

Imagine... ever present.

Imagine.

The world broke my heart,
And You filled it with Grace.

I loved, and was loved, "because of",
And You made me... Love itself.

I was exiled and alone,
And You embraced me...

Until I and the world vanished.

I was drowning in sorrow,
And You immersed that sorrow...

In the Ocean of Bliss.

It hurt to be alive as "me",
And You made me no longer one alive...

But Life Itself.

Looking within, I found my Self,
And then, at my Heart's behest...

Found My Self, again, as You.

LOVE AND SURRENDER

These days, with more behind than ahead,
I do not yearn to solve the Mystery of Life,
Or come to "enlightenment" or "awakening".

Those words long ago lost all meaning,
And the Great Mystery has proven,
Beyond all doubt, Unknowable.

These days, I Cherish two things:

The Sacred Presence in The Heart,
That Fullness, Completion, and Bliss,
Which Illumines the Experience of Being.

Love.

And the Enlivened Serenity of a mind,
Though ever awash in Wonder,
Surrendered to Not Knowing.

Love... and Surrender.

Having these,
What care is there of attainment,
Or "levels" of enlightenment?

Having these,
What care is there for states of being,
Created and sustained in conditionality?

Having these,
How can one bear arid discourses,
Seeking to prove this "Truth" or that?

Having these,
What "spiritual desire" can arise,
Save...

Love's desire to Bless.

I've grown so very weary of all else "spiritual".

These days, with more behind than ahead,
This Mystery within a Mystery is content,
To breathe in Love, and breath out Surrender.

A GESTURE OF LOVE

It was a Gesture of Love,
Not a skill "learned",
This turning to face The Beloved.

In the Garden of the Beloved

I could not grasp, or She would flee,
I could not seek to hold and sustain,
Or The Friend would vanish.

She taught me this, Herself.

It was a gentle turning of Attention,
A movement of Affection, within,
Until "I" could no longer be found…

And yet… Aliveness Shone.

It was not enough to come to this place,
Where, unable to find myself,
"I" became Vast and Limitless.

For this "I", as well,
However subtle the feeling,
Had to Vanish.

There, at that Juncture,
I moved from thoughtful investigation,
To Feeling enquiry…

Where no "I" was found…
I Felt what Was,
And Rested there, ever more deeply.

The mind's capabilities exhausted,
I Felt for that which was there,
Before ever I learned…

"Who" I was,
"What" I was,
"How" I was.

Before ever I knew,
What "I" meant,
And "I" and "thou" arose.

The Beloved awaited there,
To Vanish with me,
Into the Great Mystery…

My own Shining Aliveness,
Before this twinkling Dream ever sparkled…
From the Infinitely faceted diamond of…

Stop now… Shhhhhhh… and Feel.

IN RAINS OF WONDER

There are those who wander,
Outside the walls of religion,

Belief, and descriptions of "Truth",
No longer sufficing,

Faith in a distant Heaven,
Having lost its allure.

 In the Garden of the Beloved

They do not condemn the walled,
Who hold to belief or faith,

But embrace those who dwell there,
Holding them dear as Friends.

Only... they cannot live therein,
Having come, instead,
To a Love of the Wilderness,
And the Great Mystery... Undefined.

For it is there, in The Unknown,
That Her Silent Voice whispers.
Not in words "about", or "descriptions of",
But in the Intimacy of Direct Experience.

If one must speak of Truth,
It is, for them, Her Felt Presence,
Which stills the tongue of the mind,
Emptying in Fullness, both knower and known.

Love is there, in the Wilderness,
Where Lover and Beloved Vanish.

Fullness and Completion embrace you,
With nothing having been acquired.

Wisdom Shines like a Sun,
Everything having been forgotten.

And Benediction Showers, without cause,
Save... the simple fact of existing.

And yet, so few are moved to wander forth,
From the shelter of belief and "knowledge",
And stand naked beneath The Infinite Mystery,
Drenched… in Rains of Wonder.

MEDITATION

Is it a "practice" to Remember The Beloved?
Is recalling Her Perfume a "method"?
Does Loving Her take "will and discipline"?

What would I *do* to win Her Love,
When She Shines Causelessly,
In the Wellspring of the Heart?

Where would I *go* to find Her,
When She is ever Within,
Waiting… in the Kingdom of Heaven?

So it is with "Meditation", as I know it,
A gentle turning, in Love and Longing,
A falling Within, into Her arms.

Like one falling asleep,
All is given up in delightful Surrender,
And I am simply "taken".

Unable to discern,
In that timeless Dissolution,
Where She or I begin and end.

In the Garden of the Beloved

Lover and Beloved Vanished…
Yet Alive in that Embrace…
As Life Itself.

WHAT WAS THAT, AND WHAT IS THIS?

I am but an old beggar, bent and weary,
At the gate of the spiritual marketplace,
Asking of all who enter or leave,
"Sir, madam… please, can you tell me,
What was that… and what is this"?!

A beggar at the gate,
Not sitting "in front of", teaching,
Asserting, like those in the stalls within,
For I know less with each breath,
Asking, rather, with each heartbeat,…
"What was that, and what is this"?

What was that Nonexistent Existence,
In which all things and I Vanished,
And the Dream of Dreams,
The Heart's Deepest Desire,
Remained.

"What was that"?

Was it the Heaven, within, that Jesus spoke of?
Was it the Paradise of The Beloved's Sufis?
Was it the Atman that the Hindus speak of?
Was it God, as many understand the word?
Or was it simply… a psychosomatic anomaly?

A beggar at the gate,
Not sitting "in front of", teaching,
Not asserting, like those in the stalls within,
For I know less with each heartbeat,
Asking, rather, with each breath…

"What was that, and what is this"?

What is this touch of Nonexistent Existence,
That remained after manifest existence returned;
A Comforter, a Teacher, a Benediction,
A Wellspring of Perfection without opposite,
At the Heart of this imperfect vessel.

"What is this"?

Is it the Holy Spirit, that Jesus spoke of?
Is it The Beloved, The Friend, of the Sufis?
Is it the Bliss of the Atman, that the Hindus speak of?
Is it the Divine Presence of those who believe in God?
Or… is it simply, a psycho-somatic anomaly?

A beggar at the gate,
Not sitting "in front of", teaching,
Not asserting, like those in the stalls within,
For I know less with each passing season,
Asking always, in each moment's dissolution…

"What was that, and what is this"?

Long ago I ventured into the marketplace,
Only to be driven back by the terrible din,
Of ten thousand voices asserting,
Declaring with certitude and authority,
Ten thousand interpretations of "Truth".

Now, at last, I am leaving my station at the Gate,
No longer able to see clearly those who pass by,
Or hear their ten thousand "guesses",
My fingers calloused by touching,
Ten thousand feet in gratitude.

After a lifetime of questioning,
I have come to a certitude of my own,
That while thousands teach what they "know",
Only a handful, it appears, "Know",
That... and This.

Though the mind persists in asking,
I Live now Surrendered to Not Knowing,
Having discovered that like myself,
Those who "Know" of That and This,
In Experience, beyond concept and theory...

"know" nothing...

WAITING

How do the poems come?

I leave the door open,
Keep the kettle of Love and Surrender on the boil…

And Wait for The Poet to arrive.

THIS LOVER CANNOT BE CONVINCED

This Lover cannot be convinced, lawyerly,
That "Consciousness is all there is",
Or any such thing…

Nor do I care.

A physics "debate" on the nature of "reality",
However diamond-like the exposition,
However seemingly irrefutable…

Is a spoonful of dirt in my mouth.

This Lover desires the Wine of Longing,
The Intoxication of Dissolution,
The Rapture of Union…

Not a dissertation that seeks to "prove".

In the Garden of the Beloved

I do not seek knowledge… "about",
From the mind of another,
But the Direct Experience "of"…

In the immediacy of Existence, Now.

The knowledge of those who came before,
Debated among 10,000 schools,
Is valued only to the extent that it serves…

The Blossoming of the Heart, Now.

This Lover longs for wordless Benediction,
Not a "convincing" construct of logic and reason,
Leading to a "conclusion" of the mind…

A half-empty glass of tepid water.

The mind-bound declare this a childish emotionalism,
The stance of those unable to comprehend,
Born of a wounded need for psychological healing…

A dualistic View for the simple-minded.

But this Lover, too, used discernment and discrimination,
Only discarding them when their purpose was served,
Words, concepts, and logical constructs…

Having reached the end of their utility.

There, I revel, instead,
In Wordless Wonder of the Unknowable,
And speak of that which cannot be spoken of…

The Ineffable Sublimity of the Great Mystery.

A Love not by Lover given,
Or from Beloved received,
But rather…

The end of Lover and Beloved.

In which the "meaning" of the word "Love" Vanishes,
And only Experience remains,
An Experience had, but by no one, of…

FELLOWSHIP OF THE HEART

It matters not if you follow the cross,
Or the crescent moon,
The Buddha,
Or Zoroaster,
Whether a nondualist,
Or a Lover of the deities,
One of deep, abiding faith,
Or… one who simply does not know.

The only attribute of consequence,
In those to whom I am drawn, these days,
Is the Quality of the Heart.
Whether…
When you can,
You seek to Bless,
And when you cannot…
You strive, at least, to do no harm.

All else is dross, to this one, at least.
For I value the Fellowship of the Heart,
Above the community of belief and knowledge,
Esteeming not the outer peripheral,
But Cherishing the Inner Essential,
Eschewing "spiritual" stature,
And holding fast to those in whom I find...

Honesty, Humility, and the Simplicity of Love.

HEART AND MIND

Some seek Liberation from the pain of being "someone",
Some seek Illumination with the Inner Radiance,
The most fortunate among us, ache for both...

Liberation... and Illumination,
Freedom from bondage to the painful contraction of selfhood,
Living imbued with Bliss of our Essence, no longer veiled.

Those who seek Liberation from the knot of egoic contraction,
Arrive, if they are Blessed, at the Vanishing of that felt sense,
And feel, where "I" existed, a Serene Emptiness.

Those who long for Illumination with the Bliss of their Essence,
Come, if they are Blessed, to the ever-available presence,
Of the Fullness, Completion, and Bliss....

How tragic, though, for the felt sense of "I" to have vanished,
And the Serene Emptiness that remains to remain only Empty.
Unfilled by Richness and Warmth of The Inner Radiance.

Or how tragic, as well, for presence of The Inner Radiance,
Ever available to the inward turning of Attention,
To arise to a suffering "I", writing in inner pain.

And so, when using the mind to seek Liberation from "I",
Entwined in endless concepts, theories and conjecture,
Consider, my friend, the counsel of the Heart's Longing.

And when moving in Longing in search of your Heart's Desire,
Aching with the whole of your being for "Something Wonderful",
Consider, my friend, the counsel of the discerning mind.

And if, through Grace, "I" should vanish from Awareness…
May the Serene Emptiness, where "I" once reigned,
Be Filled with that Radiance beyond words to describe.

And if, through Grace, The Inner Radiance Shines within…
May it Shine within Serene Emptiness, free of the suffering "I",
No longer sharing interiority with the intercessor self.

For the Heart's Desire is not simply Liberation from individuation,
Or Illumination with The Mystery that is the Heart's Desire,
But to Dance in and as that Freedom, Illumined…

With Fullness, Completion, and Bliss.

THE STILL, SOFT VOICE

If you don't follow your Heart,
You'll end up in the voluntary prison,
Of another's path.

In the Garden of the Beloved

You'll pour your unique Blossoming,
Into the Experience and interpretation,
Of one long dead.

Or so you will think.
For in truth, the words of the one long dead,
Will most likely have long been lost.

Altered over time by those who followed,
And thought "about" an Experience,
Which was not their own.

Or altered by followers whose Experience,
Though a Blossoming unique from the founder's,
Was poured like new wine into the old bottle.

Walk any path, if you're Heart moves you.
Love and revere teachings and teachers.
But Revere, above all, the still, soft voice…

Of your own Heart.

FRIGHTENING AT FIRST

It was frightening at first,
Not seeing eye-to-eye,
With the Great Traditions.

Agreeing with the essential experiential,
But "interpreting" differently,
In that…

I interpreted not at all.

Not interpreting our experience,
What is left to us,
But Experience alone.

Before the voice within utters a word,
Or the inner eye imagines a form,
For the Formless and Ineffable.

While the Great Traditions "know",
What, why, and how,
I know nothing of anything…

Except this Experience of Being.

What I call Bliss is there.
But is it what is meant by Ananda?
Everyone speaks differently of it.

There is no longer the felt sense of "I".
But is that what is meant by moksha?
Everyone speaks differently of it.

This teaching says this,
That teaching says that,
And I am left wondering…

Not that it really matters.

For I do not need "knowledge",
Or "understanding",
To live in the Embrace…
Of this Unfathomable Mystery.

No matter what befalls me,
Whatever weather rages through the Sky,
Of conditionality and circumstance…

I am Held, Always.

The Beloved dwells in my Heart,
And holds me… from Within,
And I rest in Fullness and Completion…

Whatever one might call that.

DON'T STOP

When I enquired with the intellect,
And discovered myself undiscoverable,
I did not stop in the knowledge,
Of what I was not.

For what I am not, is not what I am.

However Serene that Emptiness,
However Peaceful that Vast Unlocatability,
It did not fulfill my Heart's Desire,
Being still on the far frontiers…

Of the Kingdom of Heaven.

There… at that fateful juncture,
I did not plant a flag and declare the summit,
Or give name and form to the Ineffable,
But abandoning words, concepts, and imaginings…

Fell headlong into the Heart…

Where the Serene Emptiness of Liberation,
Was Illumined with Fullness, Completion, and Bliss,
And my mind, myself, and the world lost…
I found Heaven…

In the Arms of The Beloved.

Drowning in the Depths of Her Eyes,
Knowledge… which had served so well,
In bringing me to that Far Shore,
Vanished, like so many grains of salt…

In the Ocean of Fathomless Wonder.

WHERE HAVE YOU BEEN?

At the time, it seemed horrific,
But looking back now…

I cherish the day I failed,
Inadequate, Incapable,

In the Garden of the Beloved

The day I was Defeated,
Utterly, Completely,

The day I abandoned forever,
All hope of victory,

And Surrendered,
Falling where I stood,

Only to find…
In the ashes of Catastrophe,

The face of The Beloved,
And Her Beautiful Voice, sighing…

"Where have you been?
I've been waiting".

LOVE'S INWARD TURNING

Turn Attention inward, my friend,
Not with the mind…

But with the Heart.

The mind may bestow "knowledge",
Of what you are not.

But the Heart will bring you,
The "Experience" off what you Are.

For the Heart's Unbearable Longing,
Is "of" that which is Longed for.

Resting there, in the Heart's Desire,
The Beloved will inhabit you so fully,

That where She ends and you begin…
Will no longer be discernible,

And Lover and Beloved will Vanish,
In the Rapture of their Embrace.

THE HEART

At first the Great Teacher thought not to speak,
For the nature of their Experience,
Was ineffable and inexpressible.
This was Great Wisdom.

But compelled by their Friends to speak,
They uttered words, against their better judgment,
Words and concepts to point beyond both.
This was Great Compassion.

How much clarity was conveyed?
How much confusion?
Their mind may have considered the odds,
But their Heart considered only the suffering of others.

Thankfully, or not, the Heart won the day.

And we, who came after,
And read the countless words,
The countless interpretations,
The countless additions and modifications…

We, like the Great Teacher,
Have only our Hearts to follow,
Traversing a breadcrumb trail,
That leads in 10,000 directions.

Heart and Mind,
And Intuition born of both,
Guide us on our Journey,
Not to a final "enlightenment"…

But along a path of Endless Enlightening.

INWARD TURNING

I did not find it in text on a page,
However much the words evoked the inner shimmering.
This is not to say that I did not read.

I did not find it in the eyes of my teachers,
However much they emanated Benediction.
This is not to say that I did not meditate with them.

I did not find it in the Beauty of outward objects,
Although they gave rise to that Sweet Welling Up.
This is not to say that I did not Love Beauty.

I did not find it...
In any object or experience "outside" myself.
This is not to say that I did not Love this Dream of form.

This is only to say
That the Kingdom of Heaven was,
For me...

Within.

So much in the Manifest World evoked the Love Within.
But it was the turning inward of wandering Attention,
That brought the Wanderer...

Home.

In a quest for Heaven,
That included both Heart and Mind,
The two entered the Inner Gate...

And Vanished.

How could I have known,
That it was myself that I sought,
My own nature as Formless Pure Being.

Before ever "I" existed.

And the Ecstasy of Heaven?
The Unalloyed Ecstasy,
Of my own Pure Being.

In the Garden of the Beloved

Heaven…
Not a place,
But an Experience.

In which Inner and Outer,
Within and Without,
And the Wanderer himself…

Vanish.

JEWELS

My Heart is a satchel of jewels,
Some from Hinduism
Some from Buddhism,
Some from Sufism,
Some from Christianity…

Some from Paths long forgotten.

In each of these Paths,
Mystics have arisen,
Who transcended the religiosity,
Inherent in each 'ism,
And found, as the founders had…

The jewel which gave birth to each Path.

Not the description of "reality",
The prescriptions and proscriptions,
The admonitions of thus and such,
Or culture and theology,
Accrued over ages, and codified.

The jewel which gave birth to each Path
Was, before the arising of words...
A Subjective Experience,
Prior to interpretation and description,
But clothed, eventually, in...

Concepts, theory, and conjecture.

My Heart is a satchel of jewels,
Shining in wordless Glory,
Which, though found upon this Path or that,
Are not "of" any Path,
Or description of "Truth".

How laughable, this notion of "Truth",
The diverse descriptions of "reality",
The many Paths held as Absolute,
Above all others,
And fought for, so viciously.

My Heart is a satchel of jewels,
Which, once fallen "Within",
Lose the coloration of the Paths,
Upon which I found them,
For where Formlessness Shines as Form...

All colors vanish into… White.

THE WINTER YEARS

Entering the "Winter" years, as I am,
Ever more aware of the lowering sun,
I have increasing affection and gratitude,
For the simple fact of existing.

What a mystery, and proof of Grace…
That although I remain, now, as I was in youth…
Wounded, broken, and far from perfection,
She remains ever-near in my Heart…

The Tavern of The Beloved.

There, the weary Vagabond, Attention
Finds Rest and Nourishment,
Healing and Blessing,
And languishes… Besotted by Her eyes.

I hope to die there, when my time comes,
Asleep in an upper room,
Oblivious in Surrender,
Bottle still in hand.

Or perhaps I may drop like a stone,
Here, on the dance floor,
Surrounded by Friends of the Heart,
While spinning in Wonder and Ecstasy.

Or it may be that sitting at the bar…
I will simply rest my head one day,
Unable to hold it up any longer,
Having gazed, Lovingly, so very, very long…

At the Beautiful Innkeeper.

WHAT IS THIS?

Perhaps what happened that day,
When space, time, and "I" vanished,
Was just a psycho-physiological anomaly?

Perhaps this Exquisite Bliss,
That was felt thereafter, Shining in the Heart,
Is also simply a psycho-physiological anomaly?

I've no idea, truly.

Does it shock you,
That living as this Experience,
Day to day,
Moment to moment,
Breath to breath…

I "know" nothing "about" it?

It makes my mind shudder, as well,
Though my Heart dances like a Fool, in Ignorance.

In the Garden of the Beloved

My advaitic friends interpret it one way,
Describing with great certainty and clarity,
Citing this authority or that.

Is it simply an "effect" of residing as "That"?

My Devotee friends speak of it otherwise,
Describing with great certainty and clarity,
Citing this authority or that.

Is this Bliss the Presence of God?

I heard a voice,
When the world and "I" returned that day,
Saying, "I am here for you, Always!"
And felt, through the Whole of my Being,
That Absolute Assurance.

Who uttered those words?

So many questions,
So many answers,
From so many quarters…

And everyone… so certain and assured.

I know only this…
That Formless Pure Being,
Is worthy of the name "Heaven",
And this Bliss, Shining ever-available in the Heart,
Is worthy of being called the "Divine Presence".

But interpreting and describing…
These are wholly unnecessary,
And best left to those mind-bound souls,
Who care of such things,
Move by a desperate need to "know".

I know only that this Presence… Is,
That although it Shines in the Heart,
It has no center or periphery,
And that it is a touch, alloyed,
Of Heaven's Unalloyed Ecstasy.

Does it shock you,
That living as this Experience,
Day to day,
Moment to moment,
Breath to breath…

I "know" nothing "about" it?

It makes my mind shudder, as well,
Though my Heart dances like a Fool, in Ignorance.

But now… now I will stop writing,
Of Heaven, and Bliss,
And fall headlong…
Heartlong…
Into…

LET ALL BE FREE

Thank God we are all free,
Free to follow our Heart,
Even if, in the eyes of others…
We walk the path of the Fool.

Free, no matter the shouting zealots,
Chasing us along our Way,
"Teaching", with such certainty and authority,
What is right and wrong with our view…

Right and wrong with our Experience...
Based on… theirs,
And their interpretation,
And their subsequent descriptions of…

"Truth".

Or worse, still…
The interpretations and descriptions,
Of those who came before,
And into whose old jars, new wine is poured.

Deafened by the crass cacophony,
Of the "spiritual" marketplace,
I ran, as fast as my Heart would carry me,
And wandered off… alone.

Alone…
But with this Benediction Shining in my Heart,
The goal of their prescriptions and proscriptions,
Their renunciations and disciplines.

And yet…
I did none of those.

Alone…
With Fullness and Completion Shining,
But no knowledge or understanding,
Of this Great Mystery.

For my enquiry,
Was of the Heart.

Thank God we are all free,
Free to follow our Heart.

Along the way,
I met Nowists.
"All there is, is Now".
Yes… but Romans also built a bridge, then.

Along the way,
I met Thatists.
"Thou art 'That' alone".
Truly? Where do "I" begin and end?

Along the Way,
I met Deists.

"May you come to know God".
Yes... may all come to know The Beloved.

All are true.
All are partialities.
Mere stances taken,
In relationship to...

The Unknowable...
The Unfathomable...
The Ineffable Sublimity...
Of The Great Mystery.

Thank God we are all free,
Free to follow our Heart.
Even if, in the eyes of others,
We walk the Fools path.

Let all be free.
All is as God wills it.

BECAUSE OF

If I was a Perfected Being,
This Grace would make sense
To those who say it arises
From virtue and merit...
"Because of".

Even my Beloved Baba
Said it was due to past lives
Lived in renunciation
And spiritual disciplines,
Hearing which…

I cried.

For it would not then be Grace,
Would it,
But merely a worthless trinket,
Born of conditionality,
"Because of".

That being so…
It would not be possible,
Even to discard it in a sewer,
For the sewer, feeling itself defiled
Would hurl it back… insulted.

BOB

I don't know what this is, truly…
This Warmth in the Heart,
This Bliss bubbling up from the wellspring of Being,
This Radiance that Heals and Blesses,
And intoxicates myself… and others.

In the Garden of the Beloved

Confused by the chaos of "spirituality",
The vast and varied descriptions of "Reality" and "Truth",
The stories of who, what, when, where, why, and how,
The do's and don'ts, all stated with such certitude and authority,
I find the mind simply… Stopped.

I sit, breathing Bliss, unable to feel "myself" anymore.
But have no "knowledge" about the nature of this Experience,
No description born of this tradition or that,
No cosmology or theology at all, to wrap it in,
I have only…

This Experience.

And so, at one point, I said to a Friend,
"I really shouldn't be meditating with you.
Or in any way behaving as a 'Murshid' or Guide.
For unlike all who speak with certitude and authority,
I have no 'idea' what any of this is, or what it means".

"No concepts, theories, or conjecture,
To describe the indescribable.
No constructs of logic or reason,
To create a village of understanding, belief, or faith,
In this Wilderness of the Great Mystery.

I have only… this Experience of Being".

My Friend replied…

"And that is the Treasure you can't help sharing.
Don't cringe at the word 'teacher',
Or the ways in which others teach;
Even those ways born of ancient lineage,
Held in respect and reverence".

"For when the glories of spanda,
The dance of Shiva and Shakti,
Stream out of your sparkling eyes,
Your delighted face, your every gesture,
The word 'teacher' loses all meaning…"

"And teaching gushes forth to nourish everything in its path".

"An Experience whose Beauty is beyond expression,
Like standing in a shower of Blessings,
Like soaking in a pool of Grace,
Like sunbathing in Healing Light,
Beyond all imagination… a 'Good' thing".

"So come now… let's be simple-minded, you and I,
And allow the realization of the Heart's Desire,
And the enjoyment of Ineffable Sublimity,
Inherent in the Vanishing of the enjoyer,
As reason enough to Dissolve together in Bliss".

"Why do you trouble yourself", he said,
"With why and wherefore,
With thoughts of what should be said or done…
Or not said or done,
When only this Presence is required"?

"Put 'knowledge' aside,
And all that cosmic hoo-hah that troubles you so".

"If this Grace is real,
It will Bless us,
Even if we call it... Bob,
And haven't a clue what it is,
Or what it means".

"Is it not more important,
To *have* this Experience,
Than to understand anything at all,
Or be able to speak in any way,
'About' it"?

My Friend was right,
And we continued in our Enjoyment,
And in time he became,
Effortlessly, always...
As he put it, so irreverently...

"Bobbed out".

SURRENDER CAME

Surrender... came.

It was not something "done",
Not a decision made,
Or a strategy employed,

To come to the Heart's Desire.

Not that I hadn't "tried" to Surrender,
And every other stratagem,
Finding them all, to my utter dismay…
Utterly useless.

Surrender just… came.

Not as a hallmark of Victory,
But rather… the fruition of Defeat,
A flowering, fierce and Absolute.
The death gasp of Hope and Faith.

Even a whisper of Hope remaining,
And I would have struggled on,
To create and sustain in Conditionality…
That which I longed to be without Condition.

There, in that Desert of Defeat,
I remained… and remained…
Until the last vestiges of Hope and Faith,
Fell from me like ashes.

What Wonder to discover there,
Where even demons will not go,
That… Faithless, and without Hope…
Longing remained.

Only now, no longer anywhere to go,
No longer anything to be done,
No longer anything to refrain from doing,
Exhausted, Fully and Completely.

And so… "I" fell…
Head and Heart…
Into the Wellspring of Longing,
Here… in the Cave of The Heart.

And only then, sinking ever more deeply,
Came to Longing's Source…
In the Ocean of Pure Being, where…
Through Surrender's Unimaginable Grace…

"I" drowned… in the arms of The Beloved.

KNOWING NOTHING

I could never explain to anyone,
What it was that I Longed for.
I could never explain,
Even to myself.

It wasn't just an emotional thing,
Or some object of mental curiosity,
It was something of both, and far, far more,
Across the Whole of Being.

It was there, always,
The Ancient Ache of the heart,
The relentless quest of the mind,
The furrowed brow of Wonder.

Longing.

When Longing was Fulfilled, I could never explain,
What it was that had happened,
Or the nature of that which Shone thereafter,
Effortlessly, always, in the Locus of the Heart.

Spiritual academics had many explanations,
Of both Longing and Fulfillment.
But those descriptions fell far short,
Of the Kingdom of Heaven, or the Hearts Lingering Radiance.

And so I sat, and sit, in Experience,
With no knowledge of "what" is Experienced,
For all of the explanations I have heard,
Seem to me so much concept, theory, and conjecture.

Authorities abound, emphatic, full of certitude,
On "enlightenment", "awakening", more so, or less so.
The unique expressions of those who have come before,
And experienced… Something.

I keep to myself, and avoid the "spiritual marketplace",
That cacophony of screaming vendors,
Screaming at each other, and all who pass by,
The nature of "Truth".

I sit on the porch with my puppy,
And watch the branches sway,
Dissolving in Golden Translucence.
What is that Light?

I've no "idea".

In the Garden of the Beloved

I sit and Vanish, along with the world,
As Ananda wells up, flooding the Experience of Being,
Dissolving manifest form, in the Ecstasy of Formless Being.
What is this "Ananda"?

I've no "idea".

This is not enough for many of my friends,
Who seek to understand that which is beyond understanding,
Who seek to Know that which cannot be Known,
Who seek to experience what is only experienced…

With the Vanishing of the Experiencer.

THE SWEETEST JOY

Fullness, Completion, and Bliss,
Are to The Beloved as wetness is to water,
Or heat to fire.

She Shines, Radiant like a sun,
In the locus of the Heart,
And one rests in Ineffable Sublimity.

But the Sweetest Joy,
Beyond that of our "Subjective Grace",
Is when She Floods the Heart…

Of another.

MAKE NO MISTAKE

Oh, make no mistake,
There is no "enlightened" or "awakened" one here,
Only a fellow Vagabond, like you.

Any seeming assertions,
Stated with seeming certainty,
Are only questions in disguise, certainly.

For Here, though the Heart is Illumined through Grace,
There is no "Knowledge" or "understanding",
Of this Great Mystery.

It's not that the Mind has been denigrated,
Or relegated by the Heart as irrelevant.
The poor fellow is simply… irremediably… Stymied.

There are times when the Unknowing,
Is more than he can bear,
And he collapses into the Heart's open arms.

Tears are shed, many sighs,
And ancient ages of frustration tearfully poured out,
To one sympathetic, but unable to see the problem.

In time, sobs diminish to whimpers,
A long sigh… a deep breath…
And the Mind's quest for knowledge is joined anew.

Ah, but he's fooling no one,
For the Futility of "Knowing" is known.

Alas... the poor fellow simply is as he is.

Heart and Mind...
The Heart, drunk on The Beloved's Wine, Full and Complete.
The Mind, though intoxicated through proximity...

Always Wondering.

There is no problem in this,
As it's all in the nature of things,
All as God Wills it.

SO MUCH FOR ENLIGHTENMENT

Even though I died, and became Heaven Itself,
And returned to life with a Heart Illumined by Grace,
I still cry, when the lion takes down the antelope,
I still rage, when I see cruelty and brutality,
I still crumble, at the suffering of others,
I still shudder, at the Immensity of this Great Mystery,
I still pray... though I doubt the existence of a Listener.

So much for "enlightenment".

It's only that the Heart remains Radiant with Bliss,
No matter the ever-changing weather,
In the sky of peripheral experience.

It's only that I no longer feel,
Here, within the field of experience,
The one who brought suffering.

And The Beloved never abandons me,
In the midst of Joy or Sorrow,
Laughter or tears.

So much for "enlightenment".

MOTHER OF SORROWS

I despise Mother for creating this world of suffering.
If She is truly the architect of creation… I stand against Her.

But… with each curse I hurl at Her,
She only claps her hands and falls over laughing.

I bite her ankle, this Mother of Sorrows, this Architect of Hell,
And she pulls me to Herself, tickling.

Snarling, kicking, giggling, all at once,
I struggle to get my hands around her throat.

"I hate you for creating this world of sorrows". I scream.

She stops tickling, stops laughing, and all of creation grows Silent.
And in the sudden Stillness She whispers…

"That is why I Love you so".

THE WHOLE BEING WAGGING

It's not enough to have arrived at effortlessly arising Bliss.
It's not enough to be imbued with powers, however dazzling.

It's not enough to feel yourself expanded as all that is.
It's not enough to feel yourself as That within which all arises.

It's not enough that others feel spiritual power emanating from
     you.
It's not enough that they swoon, declare pain gone, and blessings
     arrived.

It's not enough to have a brilliant mind, and a tongue to match.
It's not enough that thousands follow you.

It's not enough for the binding sense of self-identity to have
     vanished.
It's not enough to exist as the Emptiness that remains.

None of these things, and many other wondrous things as well, are
     enough,
If, bound by lingering residues of selfhood, you harm others.

Grasping after love, adoration, power, and treasure.
Wanting, needing, taking.

The Greatness of a teacher is not in their spiritual power,
Or powers of any kind, or eloquence, or charisma.

Greatness is the extent to which the vessel has been subsumed by
    Love,
Has become transparent, has ceased Grasping, and seeks only to
    Give.

I'm old, and weary of "selves" cloaked in spiritual glory.
But I am thankful each day for the Simple Ones I find.

What's this? My puppy has appeared, ball in mouth,
Her whole body wagging.

May those who seek Love find a human Guide,
Who greets them in Humility, Honesty, and Simplicity,
Free of the grasping "self"…

The Whole Being wagging.

WALLED VILLAGES

My Heart will not let me stay,
In the walled villages of belief,
And so the villagers shout,
As I push open the village gates:

"Without lineage, your own ignorance will guide you"!
"Without guidance, you will wander astray"!
"Without renunciation, Maya will swallow you"!
"Without a village… you will die in the Wilderness"!

In the Garden of the Beloved

For good or ill, my tribe are Wanderers,
Beneath the Infinite Vastness of the Great Mystery,
Heart and Mind journeying into the Unknown.
Our shelter against the Crushing Immensity…

Surrender.

There was a time when I cried,
"Teach me! I cannot bear the incomprehensibility!
Help me build a shelter of knowledge"!
But in response, Lightning struck…

And my ashes scattered to the Wind.

Far from the village…
Road vanished into path…
Path vanished into hillside…
Hillside vanished into Vastness…

The Known vanished into… Wonder.

IMPOSSIBLY

When I called out to Her,
She did not come to me,
And I cried,
"How can you be so cruel"?!

Driven by despair,
I sought to stop my Heart from beating,
And found it did not listen,
Nor would my breath.

I had nothing to do, it seemed,
With the functioning of this body,
My "participation" not required.
This body lived, and I...

I was.

It hurt so deeply, alive as "me",
An Ancient Pain, full of "what I was",
Qualifications and judgments,
The Great Suffering of "I".

There was a time, I thought,
When I existed before these things,
Qualifications, judgments, by others... and myself,
Had been heaped upon me.

And so I dove Within,
Back... behind... before, ever deeper,
Seeking the experience of Pure Being,
Before I knew anything of "myself".

No longer naming the many sounds heard,
I heard one nameless sound.
No longer naming the many things seen,
I saw one nameless vision.

In the Garden of the Beloved

I realized… there was no moment,
When I paused to consider what next to think,
And found, with a shock,
That that river flowed on… without me.

What, then, was I?

No longer the thinker,
What use in thoughtful consideration?
And so Attention moved from thought…
To Feeling.

To Feeling.

"I cannot know 'what' I am", I thought,
"Until I first find myself.
Until the…
I have only an idea".

What am I?
Where am I?
Where?
Where?

Attention, moving in Feeling,
Went in search Within,
For the location of "I",
And found… Nothing, Anywhere.

And yet… I was.

No "thing" was found,
No little man inside, locatable,
Perceiving, experiencing,
Living.

And yet... I was.

Resting there,
Unlocatable but Alive,
Suddenly it struck me,
And the gasping mind uttered...

"I... just... Am!"

And in that timeless instant... Poof!

Everything vanished.
I vanished.
Space and time vanished.
The world vanished.

No perceiver, only Perceiving,
But... nothing perceived!
No experiencer, only Experiencing,
But... only Experiencing experienced.

Not even "Consciousness", aware only of itself.

No God,
No Brahman,
No Emptiness,
No Self...

All words and concepts… Vanished.

Impossibly, in that Vanishing of Everything,
Unalloyed Ecstasy remained, the enjoyer… Vanished.
The Kingdom of Heaven within.
Not a place, but… Formless, Unmanifest…

Aliveness.

A Rapture so Ineffable,
The Heart's Desire Fulfilled.
In the timeless, spaceless, objectless,
And most importantly, subjectless Ecstasy…

Of Pure Being.

And when the world and I reappeared,
That same Ecstasy Shone in my Heart.
Diminished by its arising in form,
But its source… unmistakable.

Some say Bliss comes and goes,
And is not to be confused with the Absolute.
This is not my experience,
For the Ananda of Satchitananda…

Is effortlessly ever-present,
And inherent in the Dissolution of Manifestation,
A Dissolution and Bliss that impossibly…
Shines here… in the Dream of manifestation.

And I wonder, though I can never know…
Is this the Beloved of the Sufis?
Is this the Kingdom of Heaven?
Is this what Ramana spoke of?

Within… in the Radiant Locus of The Heart,
Where formlessness and form exist… at once,
Impossibly, Impossibly.
Impossibly…

But So.

THE HEART'S DESIRE

It's so easy to forget,
With all this talk of "spirituality",
Of all the many ways,
All the many paths,
All the many teachers…

All this talk of the Ground of Being,
Of Consciousness,
Of Brahman,
Of Emptiness,
Of Shiva and Shakti,
Of ParamAtman…

Of God.

In the Garden of the Beloved

All this talk of,
Liberation and Bondage,
Knowledge and Ignorance,
Awakening and Enlightenment…

Of the best path,
The greatest guru,
And the heartbreaking notion,
Of doing this,
And not doing that,
So that…

Of purification,
And perfecting,
And karma…

So easy to forget, in all of this...
To lose our way…
In words, thoughts, and concepts,

And to forget…

That our Heart's Desire,
Since the beginning of beginningless Time,
Has ever and always been…
To become Causeless, Conditionless Love,
And for that Love to Shine, always,
In the locus of our Heart.

To die as an object among objects,
In the Dream of space and time,
And reside, free… at last… of "our self",
As the Unalloyed Ecstasy of Heaven.

DRUNK

Nothing special happened here.
No great enlightenment.
No awakening.

I simply became Drunk
On The Beloved… Myself,
And forgot… "myself".

Intoxicated…
I can't remember
A "thing".

No sage here,
Or wise counsel to be had,
From this mouth breather.

But…
I will share this Wine… this Love,
With those who hold out their Hearts.

MYSELF

I do not feel myself expanded as all that is,
A part of everything, and everything a part of me.

Nor do I feel myself as "That" within which all appears,
The Absolute, everything arising within me.

I do not feel "myself" at all.

Unless, by "I" you mean...
This.

Not a thing alive,
But... Aliveness Itself.

Formless Aliveness in samadhi,
Or Aliveness in form...

Show me that place, where one ends,
And the other begins?

Show me that place,
Where "This" begins and ends?

One thought of "This and That"...
One thought of "I" and "other"...

And Heaven and Earth are rent asunder!

LIBERATION OF THE WHOLE BEING

Until the Whole Being is Liberated,
Until the head falls into the Heart,
We have, at the least, only a cerebral freedom,
And at best, existence merely as "That".

It is one thing to understand,
Another to Know,
Another to Be.

It is one thing to be The Ocean,
Another to be a river,
And another to vanish in their merging.

We can "know" that we do not exist,
As an object in space and time,
And yet...
Feel as if we do.

The body must be released,
As well as the mind.
Every aspect of Form,
Dissolved in Formlessness,
Leaving Formless Form.

Some, imbued with powerful Shakti,
Enamoured of experience,
Often refuse to give up the experiencer,
The "enlightened" one,
And remain a powerful "person".

In the Garden of the Beloved

Blissless advaitans,
Conditioned by long sadhana,
Dismiss Ananda as mere "experience",
And lead "awakened" lives
Of cerebral aridity.

Right Understanding is essential,
And Right Relationship to,
Formlessness and Form,
Shiva and Shakti,
The Fullness of the Experience of Being.

For Form is to Formlessness,
Shakti is to Shiva,
As wetness is to water,
As heat is to fire,
And the Lover to the Beloved.

Existence as the enjoyer,
However Blissful,
Is life in the hell world,
Of ten thousand pleasures.

And existence merely as "That",
However liberating,
Has the stink of subtle duality,
The most insidious of delusions.

For neither This,
Nor That,
Have ever existed…
I Am.

MIND AND HEART

We're older now, Mind and Heart,
With less ahead of us, than behind.
All our lives we have wondered,
At this Great Matter of… Existing.
This Great Matter of Being Alive.

In our wanderings, far and wide,
We have spent time in the walled villages,
Of many traditions, many teachings.
Villages laid out this way and that,
In their expressions of "truth", "reality"…

And "enlightenment".

In each village Mind has run,
Like a starving vagrant, malnourished,
To the temples of knowledge,
To sit at the feet of the "enlightened",
Gorging voraciously…

On interpretations and descriptions,

While the Heart, having none of it,
Reveled in Bliss at the Tavern of The Beloved,
Sipping Grace, as She poured, again and again,
Until all was forgotten,
And only She and Heart remained…

Then… both Vanishing.

In the Garden of the Beloved

Each time, in the villages of tradition,
Mind would arrive, in time, at the Tavern door,
Bedraggled, forlorn, more ignorant than before.
And there, joining Heart at the bar,
Would sob to all who would listen, its tale of woe.

And in time, each time, again and again,
The two staggering drunkards, Mind and Heart,
Pushed open the village gates and wandered out;
The Heart… into Endless Wonder,
The mind…

Into the Incomprehensibility of This Great Mystery.

SURRENDER

Surrender was coming to know,
Beyond all doubt,
That I will never know.
Never…
Ever.

It was coming to see, beyond all doubt,
That unlike those with clarity of mind,
And the hopeful certitude of faith,
I would live out my life in and as…
A Great Mystery.

Although I found jewels in religions and philosophies,
That resonated with Heart and mind,
I was ultimately left wondering,
At the vast and varied differences debated,
Among the Great Traditions.

Who had decided that "truth" was thus?
Traditions within traditions.
Emphatic partialities, all, they seemed to me.
And… did it really matter to me, at all,
What "truth" was?

Was "truth" what I longed for,
Or "understanding" of the nature of "reality",
Argued with dogmatic hubris,
By mind-bound academics,
Of the vast and varied schools?

It seemed that in all but the rarest instances,
The Heart had been "thought" out of the Great Matter,
By those cherishing "knowledge of",
But lacking Direct Experience.

As the years passed, I lost clarity,
Even around what it was I sought,
Hobbled by the confusion of teachings,
Prescriptions and proscriptions…

And descriptions of "truth" and "reality".

In the Garden of the Beloved

Decades passed further,
And I watched fall from my hands,
The few shards of clarity I had garnered here and there,
Which had seemed, in their time, so "True" to me.

Trinkets of Belief once held, white-knuckled,
Against the Great Unknown,
Abandoned now…
Collapsed lean-to's against the Incomprehensible.

Stripped naked of hope,
Faith, a tattered rag, long fallen away,
"Knowledge" burned to ash,
In the fierce Heat of The Great Mystery.

Turning from all outward searching,
Into the depths of formless Being,
I searched within to see,
If anything at all was left to me.

And there found…
To my gentle surprise…
The only thing that remained;
The last vestige of the first cause…

The Longing in my Heart.

Somehow,
Impossibly…
Inextinguishable.

The Longing that had moved me,
From the very first step,
Somehow, impossibly… remaining.

And falling headlong into that Pool,
Breathing those Living Waters,
I drowned, at last, in The Heart's Desire.

Longing having been the Wellspring,
All those long, weary years,
Of that which was longed for.

The Fragrance of that which was Longed for,
Having been, all along,
"Of" that which was Longed for.

Drowned, into and as Formless Aliveness,
I returned, Alive, as form,
But drenched, thereafter, in Bliss.

Bliss…
Not coming and going, as I had read,
But effortlessly ever-present.

Who were these "awakened" ones,
Who spoke with such certainty and authority,
Of that which was not in their experience?

Bliss…
The Peace that Transcends Understanding…
Imbued with the Ecstasy of Formless Pure Being.

In the Garden of the Beloved

Rapturous, the background of experience,
Not merely Peace, Happiness, and Joy,
Which flitted erratically in the realm of causality.

Bliss...
When Attention moved outward,
The background of all Experience.

Soft, subtle, ambient...
Everywhere and nowhere,
Impossibly, both at once.

Bliss...
When Attention relaxed inward,
The Ocean of Ecstasy within which all arose.

Inherent in the tsunami of Dissolution,
Flooding the Whole of Being,
Dissolving inward and outward.

The mind too dissolute to contemplate,
What remained when "I" and the world Vanished,
Or ponder the Bliss Shining thereafter in the Heart.

Unable to cognize or articulate,
The nature of "truth" or "reality"
Recoiling from concept, theory, and conjecture...

I leave such things to those who must know.

Illumined with ever-present Bliss,
The salt doll "I" Dissolved,
I remain, as ever, Surrendered to never knowing…

Ever.

SURRENDERED

Buddha experienced what he called "enlightenment",
And at first, thought it impossible to convey.
But entreated by old friends,
Was convinced to speak.

Moved by Compassion, he struggled,
To describe his Subjective Experience,
To point the way for others,
So their suffering, too, might end.

And so with all great teachers,
And all great teachings,
Experience, Interpretation, description,
Followed by prescriptions and proscriptions.

Heaven, Nirvana, Enlightenment,
Is thus, they say.
To come to it,
Do thus, not thus.

In the Garden of the Beloved

And thus…
The many paths are born.
Many paths…
Many Ways.

First, the experience described,
It's value conveyed,
And then the Way explained,
The moon reflected in water.

If enlightenment was not described,
How would any know of it,
And why it should be sought,
Among the 10,000 allures.

If a Way is not shown,
A Way cannot be followed,
To the end of suffering,
And the advent of Satchitananda.

Buddha interpreted his experience thus,
Shankara thus, Mahavir thus,
Lao Tzu thus, Bodhidharma thus,
And on and on… and on.

Experience,
Interpretation,
Expression.

And in most instances,
So much more, heaped upon the essence;
Entire cosmologies formed,
Complex descriptions of "reality".

So many teachers,
So many teachings,
All expressing The Way,
With certitude and authority.

And those who seek desperately,
A mirroring of clarity and context,
Search the words of those dead and living,
For some reflection…
Of their own unique Experience of Being.

They seek clarification of confusions,
Context, understanding… deepening,
Regarding the Great Mystery unfolding…
In their own unique Experience of Being.

Here and there they find affinity,
In the experiences of others,
The interpretations of others,
The expressions of others.

Wherever I searched,
In the teachings of others,
I found only pieces, more or less so…
Of my own unique Experience of Being.

In the Garden of the Beloved

Among friends, as well, met along the Way,
I saw the taking of this, and discarding of that
As each piece fit, more or less so…
Their own unique Experience of Being.

Gods and Goddesses,
Masters, Gurus, Saints,
Each reflecting this facet or that,
Of this incomprehensible Diamond.

Each a beautiful reflection,
Each a useful teaching,
Each…
A partiality.

A partiality.

Finding no refuge whole and complete,
In this view or that,
I fell down where I stood, Homeless…
In the Infinitude of incomprehensibility.

Surrender…

Far from the Village of the Known,
Road vanished into path,
Path vanished into hillside,
Hillside vanished into Vastness,
Vastness vanished into…

My Sat Guru,
My Heart,
Could offer no guidance,
Except…

Surrender…

Complete,
Absolute,
Across… the… Whole… of… Being…

Surrender…

The mind having reached the end of its ability,
Too intoxicated, too drunk with Amrita,
To understand or comprehend… anything at all.

Surrender…

To a Heart Shining, beyond all understanding,
With the Ecstasy of Heaven,
And Filled to overflowing, with Causeless Love.

Surrender…

To Grace… Unearned, Unmerited,
Born of the simple fact,
Of Existing…

Surrendered.

TOUCHING THE HEM OF HER SARI

There are those among us who say,
The body should be viewed as an obstacle,
As merely a sack of blood and bones,
And aspirants to "God" should not touch,
Even the hem of a woman's garment.

I can only say that throughout my life…

In the eyes of those I have Loved,
Even in moments lost in passion's ecstasy,
I never saw simply the beauty of the woman,
I both Loved, and desired.

I saw the Mystery she was, before her birth;
The shock in the eyes of the newborn;
The twinkling innocence of the little girl;
The adolescent, seeking love and belonging;
The mother, selfless, gentle, compassionate;
All… awash in Love.

I saw the wrinkled face of my mother…
Heard her last breath, sighing,
And saw those beautiful eyes closing…
After Dancing, so long, in the Dream of Life.

All of these beings, I saw before me,
In the timeless moment of Love's embrace,
In the eyes of those I have encountered,
Whom I both Loved, and desired.

In each of this life's relationships,
The Beloved staring back at me,
My Mother, sister, daughter, lover… Myself,
In the eyes of those I both Loved, and desired.

How could I, why would I,
Ever "renounce" as obstacle,
The Presence of The Beautiful One,
In the eyes of those I both Loved, and desired…

There… in the Eyes of God.

THE JOURNEY TO HEAVEN

We begin simply hearing of it, and disbelieving.
How could something so Wonderful be true,
When all we've ever known…
This body, this world,
And ever-changing conditionality…
Point to its impossibility?

Notions of Liberation from the suffering of "I",
And even more so the advent
Of Unalloyed Ecstasy…
Are thought, by the Mind,
To be delusions.

In the Garden of the Beloved

But deep within,
In The Realm of The Heart,
We cannot escape the strange Longing
That will not be extinguished,
For that which cannot be put into words.

At some point, if we are Blessed...

We turn to seek Ourself,
Feeling our way back... back...
Behind all that appears to us...
Struggling to locate our Source.

What am I?
Where am I?
Where?
Where?

Where is the seer,
The perceiver,
The knower,
The experiencer?

At some point, if we are Blessed...

The Fragrance of Heaven
Wafts across our path,
Here... in the realm of Experience.
And is recognized,
In the very instant of its appearing,
Though never before known to us,
As our Heart's Desire.

This is the Fragrance…
Of our own Pure Being,
And a sign that we have traveled, at last,
From the far frontiers…
Into the borderlands of Heaven.

Now our course is moved, at every turn,
In pursuit of this fleeting Fragrance,
Back, back, behind all that appears to us,
And we are guided, in the truest sense…
By our Sat Guru.

We "remember" the Feeling of It,
Not with our mind,
But with our Whole Being.
We Feel our way to Heaven,
Back… back…
Behind all that appears to us.

At some point, if we are Blessed…

The Fragrance begins to arise
Not only in conscious moments of inward turning,
But spontaneously, and we are taken unawares.
Having begun in soliciting, we are solicited.

At some point, if we are Blessed…

In the Garden of the Beloved

All that appears to us becomes apparitional,
And we... as well,
And we see... far off...
The City on The Hill,
Wherein lays the Temple.

At some point, if we are Blessed...

The Fragrance of the Temple's Incense, Ananda,
Surrounds us always, breathed in, and out,
Inherent in, and inseparable from,
The turning inward of Attention.

At some point, if we are Blessed...

The Fragrance of Ananda
Takes up residence, paradoxically, in our Heart;
Here... in this Locus of Experience
That is our Manifest Being.

Now, so close to Formless dissolution...

An impossible mystical alchemy
That transcends the laws of duality,
Brings about the Experience,
Of Formlessness in Form.

Only the smallest distance remaining...

Only a thought,
Between "I" and Utter Dissolution,
The continued inward turning,
And ever-increasing Ecstasy,
Brings us to the door of the Holy of Holies.

And then…
if we are Blessed…

Poof!

AUTONOMY

Autonomy… so essential,
Almost…
Almost above all else.

For even if we have great longing,
Without which, we are mere thinkers,
But lack autonomy…

Our longing can be poured into the mold,
Of another's experience,
And more dangerously, still…
Their interpretation of their experience.

Buddha, Jesus, Ramana,
Any historical or contemporary teacher…
Their experience was theirs,
And their interpretation, as well.

In the Garden of the Beloved

Ancient lineages assert,
With fierce certitude,
Their unquestionable authority.
But these, too… are interpretations.

We can revere and honor,
The teachings of others,
And the many blessings they hold,
Without becoming subservient to them.

We can take what resonates,
And leave what does not, respectfully,
However revered the teacher,
However ancient the lineage.

We can take and leave, as well,
Our *own* interpretations
Of the experience we have come to,
And what it all means.

Head and Heart, ever-open, ever-free,
We need not seek to grasp or hold,
Or plant a flag along the way,
Declaring the summit attained.

In each new experience,
In each new revelation,
We dawdle for a time,
In all that is revealed.

At each new milestone,
Each new vista come upon,
We celebrate for a time,
The gifts discovered.

Until… if we are blessed,
The Unknown calls to us,
And we wander, again…
Into the Great Mystery.

We are moved,
Without intention or volition,
To walk, in Wonder and Awe,
At the glories of each ever-new step.

Autonomous and free,
Unbound by stances and views
Held by others, and…
By our self.

A SIMPLE MAN

"You must always remain a simple man,
A simple man, leading a simple life". my Baba said.

"You will not *push* yourself out.
Printing up flyers, renting a hall,
And throwing the doors open,
For all who pass by.

In the Garden of the Beloved

Those who Love will be… pulled,
And will come to take tea and chat.

You will not sit 'in front' of a group,
But only, always, 'across' from a Friend,
Fellow Lovers on the Way of the Heart…
Bathed in the Perfume of The Beloved.

You will not express, assertively,
The Grace you have received…

Rather, they will tell *you*,
When they feel its Radiance.

Only then… you may speak.

But you needn't speak,
To inform or instruct.

You needn't speak at all.

Only The Beloved's Presence is required,
To Invoke what words can never convey.

And in time, through Grace,
As you have received…

They will become… like you!

And in all of this, all of this,
You will remain, *always*…

Always…

A simple man".

And so should we all remain.

WHERE?

Friend: Ah, Nasrudin, how are you, my friend?

Nasrudin: How glorious the chrysanthemums!

Friend: Yes, they are. But I asked about you, my friend.

Nasrudin: Where do I begin and end?

THE WAY OF THE HEART

You have been Graced into the Secret Way,
The Way of the Heart.

"Understanding",
However diamond-like,
However impactful on the Experience of Being,
Will never again satisfy you.

The bee has done its job,
And the pollen of knowledge
Has been transmuted by Mystical Alchemy
Into Bliss.

In the Garden of the Beloved

Now… the bee dies,
Understanding and knowledge,
Turn from soft parchment to dust,
And you Live wide-eyed, in Awe and Wonder…

In The Great Mystery,
As The Great Mystery.

You drink from Living Waters now,
Flowing from the Wellspring of the Heart.

All is changed. All is changed.
Oh mind, oh mind, I leave you here.

Only words Wet,
Will find resonance,
In one already dampened.

The Emanation of Love,
Will only touch your Heart,
If you are already pregnant with Longing.

How will you know?
The baby will kick.

You are now… Alone,
And never again Alone.

While you may long to find
Fellow Idiots, thus imbued,
Finding none, you remain Full and Complete.

Now Your Heart
Will look Lovingly for itself
In all that is experienced,
And in all who are met.

THE HIGHEST TEACHER

One person will go to a teacher,
And the baby will kick in the womb.
Another will find only fault.

One person's mind will be illumined by a teacher's erudition,
Their diamond-like articulation.
Another will receive only empty words.

One person will sense great Bliss pouring from a teacher,
Revealing in themselves, the same Splendour.
Another will feel the teacher dry, brittle, and wooden.

One may emerge unscathed by a teacher's imperfections,
And their own naivete,
While another crashes and burns.

Each may go on to tell others of their experience,
That this is such and so,
As if it is Truth.

We simply cannot "know"
The Fullness of "Truth",
From the words or injunctions of another.

Only our Heart, the Highest Teacher,
Can tell us when to Love, for how long,
And when to come and go.

JASMINE

One cannot approach Jasmine,
Without being embraced by its Fragrance.
Likewise with The Beloved,
And Her Fragrance… Bliss.

The Sweetness is "of" Jasmine,
And Bliss "of" The Beautiful One,
As wetness is to water,
Or glistening to gold.

The Fragrance of Jasmine,
Arises only from Jasmine.
And Jasmine without Fragrance,
Is not Jasmine.

The two are One,
Fragrance not merely an "effect of",
But inherent in…
The Jasmine of The Soul.

The "two" are One.

We wander, moved by Unbearable Longing,
For the Fulfillment of our Heart's Desire,
And in a moment of Grace…

The Perfume of the Beloved wafts by.

Do we dismiss that Fragrance,
As "not Jasmine",
As merely a "transient, 'unreal' apparition",
And arrive at a Flower without attributes?

Do we declare it "Maya",
A Delusion,
A Deceit,
A "Dangerous Sweet"?

Only those who have merely "read of",
Only those merely "thinking about",
Would dismiss this Fragrance,
Never lifting their gaze to the Flower...

Never dropping,
From head to Heart,
From concept to Experience,
From "knowledge" to Love.

To each their own.
But the Lovers I cherish,
Follow the Fragrance,
Dancing, flirtatious...

Drawing them ever nearer
To Death as a Jasmine Lover,
And Life, beyond Lover and Beloved,
As Jasmine, Itself.

THE RAINS OF HEAVEN

When I wandered in search of Heaven,
I encountered villages along the way,
And inquired of each, the path to follow.

In each, a different way was pointed,
And the "correct" manner in which to walk.
And in each, a different description of Heaven.

Each description was of… something else,
Something other than my Heart's Desire,
An Ancient Memory of a Love forgotten.

When I spoke of this Love's guiding Mercy,
Bringing me one day, surely, to its Fulfillment,
They mocked my naivete, saying…

Not until…

Not until I stopped doing this, and began doing that.
Not until I renounced, and led a chaste life.
Not until I purified my impure nature.

Not until I meditated perfectly.
Not until I accrued sufficient merit.
Not until I transcended.

Not until…

Not until I saw as they saw,
Not until I understood as they understood,
Not until I experienced as they experienced.

Oh… poor villagers,
Huddled behind the walls of the known,
Fearing the Wilderness more than hell itself.

I did naught of what I was told I must,
And reveled in those things I was told I must not,
Stoned along the way by the righteous.

My Heart, Surrendered, a Captive of Love,
My Mind a Dreamer of Unimaginable Grace,
My Spirit, a Sobbing Lover in Exile.

Wherever I found myself wandering,
However "sinful" my thoughts, speech, or actions,
I felt always and everywhere… Unbearable Longing.

In each step, each breath, every heartbeat,
I walked, always, with a Heart in tears,
For Love as yet unknown, but Known.

And living thus, a Wilderness Wanderer,
With Longing, alone, the substance of my sadhana,
"I" found Her… at last…and died in Her arms.

It is not what you do, or do not do,
But the Quality of your Love and Longing,
That brings the Rains of Heaven.

Drenched, Soaking, Enraptured… I swear it.

I swear it.

THE ULTIMATE HOTTIE

Sometimes spiritual seekers seem like alcoholics,
And gurus like bartenders,
And sanghas like nightclubs,
And "God"… the Ultimate Hottie.

Alas… when satsang ends,
And the "high" wears off after a few days,
And the Ultimate Hottie stops returning our calls,
She seems nothing more than the Ultimate Tease.

Beside ourself with Grief and Longing,
We drink our way into oblivion,
And awaken, dawn after dawn,
In the arms of Maya.

Until… one morning,
Turning to gaze upon the face of Illusion,
We see, instead,
Our long lost Beloved.

It was Her all along,
Wearing Maya's makeup!
We were simply too drunk,
On the bartender's words.

LOVE ALL ALONG

It was only near the end that I realized,
After so many years,
That all I ever wanted was…
Love.

For so long, I lusted for ecstasy,
Or a long lost Shanghri La,
For Heaven,
Or "enlightenment".

But it was none of these.

When Love, without cause or condition,
Filled the Serene Emptiness,
Left when "I" vanished,
All was Fulfilled.

All was Fulfilled.

EXPRESSING THE INEXPRESSIBLE

We struggle desperately through Love,
To express in words, concepts, and metaphor,
That which cannot be expressed.

For this Grace can only be communicated,
In the Fullness of its Essence,
Through wordless Benediction, Heart to Heart…

If you can let go and fall, for just one moment,
From knowing to Wonder, head to Heart,
From concept to Experience…

And allow yourself to be "Meditated".

DOUBTS

During my Journey,
As I chased the dream of "enlightenment",
Wandering the desert of "myself" in search of Water,
I ate, drank, and breathed doubts.

Doubts about enlightenment itself,
That this felt sense of "I" would ever vanish,
Could ever vanish.

Doubts about the "enlightened" and "awakened",
So many of whom seemed to me, Delusional,
Wounded, broken, and often pathological.

Doubts about the Great Teachings,
As I encountered them along the Way,
So rife with belief, orthodoxy, and dogma.

Doubts about my ability to do and not do,
To embrace practice and technique,
To exert will and discipline.

Doubts that it was all simply a grand fairytale,
The hysterical delusions of religious types,
Or the conceptualizing of intellectuals, full of hubris.

All so very certain in faith or knowledge,
About that which I could only…
Doubt.

Now… looking back, I see…
Doubts were not the harbingers of despair,
Nor demons which hindered and harmed.

They were the shining weapons of my Honesty,
Born of fierce discernment, discrimination,
And an empiricism* that would simply… not… die.

Any view, any Expression of "Truth",
That could not withstand their onslaught,
Fell in defeat, however revered it was by others.

Doubts led me, ultimately, to The Great Mystery,
Where nothing is known,
And nothing is resolved.

They led me, after such a long Odyssey,
To where Absolute Doubt,
Turned to Absolute Surrender.

When the last breath of hope was whispered,
When all grasping ceased, for "more",
When in despair's fruition, I collapsed where I stood.

I died as a thing that existed, a thing alive,
And Remained, as Existence, Life Itself.

WHAT IS IT YOU WANT?

Is it "knowledge" you desire, of this, that, or the other,
Do you seek a "conclusion" arrived at by the mind?
Or do you struggle endlessly, as do so many,
Holding fast to belief, while nurturing tenuous faith?

Or do you long for the immediacy of Experience,
Experience that is your own, palpable and visceral,
Not merely in transient "spiritual" moments,
But always, with every breath, every heartbeat…

Filling the Experience of Being,
With Warmth and Richness,
Fullness, Completion...
And Bliss.

Knowledge is of use only as kindling for Experience,
For otherwise, like wood stored against winter's cold,
Unburned in the Hearth of the Heart's Longing,
It will not Warm and Comfort your Spirit.

Only the Heart's Flame will ignite that Fire,
Consuming, across the Whole of your Being,
The terrible contraction, the painful sense,
Of "I", separate, and alone.

Whether Consciousness is the Formless Ground of Being,
Or an endless flow of Causality arising in Emptiness,
Is of no consequence, whatsoever,
Unless such knowledge evokes Experience.

Without Longing…

You can hear all the words in the world,
And the ember of your Heart will not ignite.
You can see every "teacher du jour",
And the wellspring of your Heart will not overflow.

Without Longing…

Disciplined, you can perform 10,000 prostrations,
Recite one million "Om Mane Padme Hums",
And receive countless empowerments,
And the Sun of your Heart will not Shine.

Without Love's Unbearable Longing,
Teachings are the sound of dry bones crumbling,
The most powerful teachers, no more than mannequins,
And the highest "highs"… only memories.

Only Longing, deep, vast, and enduring,
Will water the seedling of the mind's understanding,
And reap The Heart's Desire,
From the arid fields of knowledge.

In the Garden of the Beloved

This is a matter of Mind and Heart,
Not an academic endeavor to be figured out; "gotten".
One does not "learn" the meaning of the words…
Existence, Consciousness, Bliss.

TWO HEARTS

Trees sway in the Santa Ana wind,
Dappled sunlight dances across the room.

Warm puppy in the cave beneath my desk,
Curled against my bare feet.

Coolness against my face,
The silent fan turning.

Distant cars,
Like ocean sounds.

And here, in this Locus of Form,
Right… Here…

Two hearts.

One the drummer I've known since birth,
Beating in my breast.

The other…

A shining sun,
A fluttering breeze,
A fragrant blossoming,
An overflowing wellspring,
A breathing in and out of Bliss,
Flooding the Experience of Being.

Form and formlessness,
Both... at once.

Tell me, where does one Heart end,
And the other being?

HEAVEN'S LIGHT

If I was only able to speak,
Of The Great Matter,
I would remain silent.

There is enough talking "about" in the world.
And knowledge acquired through words alone,
Is like money in a bank account,
Without the pin code of the Heart's magic.

Far more than speaking countless words...
The emanation of Grace,
And the Miracle of its Fire,
Igniting the ember in the Hearts of others...

Demands the giving of Love, Time, and Attention
To those Blessed to notice its Warmth,
And unable to live one moment longer,
In a world unlit by Heaven's Light.

A DIFFERENT PLACE

This Fullness, Completion, and Bliss,
Does not exist in the realm,
Of ever-changing conditionality,
The ever-changing weather of manifestation.

Although it Shines into that realm.

This Fullness, Completion, and Bliss,
Has nothing whatsoever to do,
With "becoming" this or that,
With "doing" or "not doing",

Nothing to do with "changing",
With "perfecting",
With starting or stopping,
With "when" or "if".

This Fullness, Completion, and Bliss,
Exists in a... "different place".
Within which, from which, as which,
Lover and Beloved arise.

Although Joy and Sorrow may ebb and flow,
Laughter and tears may come and go,
Faith and belief stand strong. or crumble...
This Presence remains, in a "different place"...

The Wellspring of The Heart.

And although Unmoved, Impenetrable,
Untouched by the ever-changing nature,
Of this Dream of Heaven and Hell,
This Fullness, Completion, and Bliss...

Illumines that Dream of opposites...

From a Different Place.

LEAN-TO

Here in the Wilderness,
Lost in The Great Unknowable,
I found myself unable to stop,
Building lean-tos.

Lean-tos of understanding,
Even if that understanding,
Was that nothing, really,
Can ever be "understood".

In the Garden of the Beloved

I could not seem to help myself,
From the innate human tendency,
To erect a shelter, however small,
From This Great Mystery.

In my life I have taken refuge,
In villages of many faiths,
Walled and well ordered,
Against the Unutterable.

So few there,
Dared come close,
To the foreboding gates,
Beyond which…

Beyond which…
All beliefs are questioned.
Beyond which…
Faith might be weakened.

Where…
In a Pathless Wilderness,
Devouring all certitude,
The "Monster" of the Unknowable roams.

I understand,
For my fear, too, was crippling.
And walking even near the gate,
I grew faint of heart, and turned away.

But in each village,
Again and again,
I would eventually approach,
And push open those Fearful Gates.

I was moved to such heroism,
Not only by the desolation of belief,
Or the withering of faith,
But by… Longing.

Longing for that,
Which remained unfulfilled,
In Heart and Mind,
Across the Whole of Being.

Longing for that which,
Unable to be articulated,
Even within myself,
Was Known, as the Heart's Desire.

An Ancient Longing,
Ancient beyond time,
For Fullness, Completion,
And… Love.

I stepped out from village walls,
And resumed, with lonely steps,
The Great Journey I'd begun,
When first… I Wondered.

In the Garden of the Beloved

I wandered forth into The Wild,
Abandoning all and everything,
With only the Fellowship…
Of my Own Beloved Heart.

Far from the village,
Road vanished into path…
Path vanished into hillside…
Hillside vanished into Vastness…

The Known vanished…
Into Wonder.

And each time, in time,
As I wandered forth,
Beneath the crushing Vastness,
Of the Infinite Heavens…

I forgot where "I" ended, and Heaven began.

And each time, in time,
As I wandered forth,
Having become indecipherable,
From the Earth upon which I sat…

I forgot where "I" ended, and Earth began.

And then…

Each time, in time…
There arose the movement of Mind,
Reaching slowly for a word,
To begin building…

A lean-to.

A lean-to of understanding,
Even if that understanding,
Is that nothing, really,
Can ever be "understood".

How does one come to the Heart's Desire,
When understanding and knowledge fail,
And lost and alone, one wanders,
From the village of the known?

How does one survive,
Much less come to Fruition,
In a Pathless Wilderness
Of Crushing Unknowability?

Surrender.
Drop that stick.
Abandon all shelter.
And Die of Exposure…

To Love.

DISSOLVING

So many voices.
So many words.
So many teachings.
So many lineages.
So many orthodoxies.
All... emphatic in their assertions.

So many pundits.
So many gurus.
So many sat gurus.
So many avatars.

Shakti empowered psychopaths.
Blissless advaitans.
Scripture-bound dogmatists.
Merit-based attainers.

So wearying.

So much to be done,
And me, without discipline.

So much to be refrained from,
And me, so enjoying it all.

So much to read,
And me, with the attention span of a gnat.

So much to be understood,
And me, never grasping.

So much merit to be accrued,
And me, holding attainment in disdain.

One day, through Grace,
It finally happened…

I drowned in the din of voices,
Teachings, teachers,
Paths, lineages,
Prescriptions and proscriptions,
Attainment of "knowledge",
Accrual of merit

The mind floating, lifeless,
Adrift without words….
The Heart fallen down,
In Absolute Surrender.

Dissolving,
In the Ocean of the Great Mystery,
The Unknowable, the Unattainable.
Abandoning both Liberation and Bondage,
Abandoning "my" self, "my" Life…

No longer able to discern,
Word from word,
Concept from concept,
Theory from theory,
Conjecture from conjecture.

In the Garden of the Beloved

Hope long vanished, collapsed in despair,
Deafened by the cacophony of voices,
Blinded by the carnival of glamors,
Straining to remember the Taste of my Heart's Desire,
The Fragrance of the Beloved, Her Ecstatic Touch…

Through the Unimagined Grace
Of Utter, Absolute Failure,
"I" quit.
Or should I say…
"I" was quit.

In Absolute Hopelessness,
In Absolute Despair,
With an exhausted last breath…

Absolute Surrender.

No enlightenment,
No realization,
No awakening,
No goal achieved,
Nothing understood,
No perfection attained.

Surrender.

And somehow,
Mysteriously,
Impossibly,
In that Quitting,
In that Surrender,
In that Giving Up…

Liberation, at last,
At last,
At last...
Not only from my self,
But from "Liberation".

Everything abandoned,
Everything...
For this Ineffably Sublime Idiocy

LOVE ALONE

I have studied the lives of the great saints,
Perfected in virtue and "spiritual" qualities...

And I am not one of those.

I have admired those with will and discipline,
Who struggle and strive so fiercely...

And I am not one of those.

I have listened to diamond-like articulations,
From those blessed with eloquence of mind...

And I am not one of those.

I have known those whose hearts are warmed,
By Faith and Hope, alive and shining...

And I am not one of those.

If Grace had not showered upon this weary Soul,
Simply because, I Am...

If Love had not Blossomed in this aching Heart,
Simply because, I Am...

I would have been lost, forever, beyond all hope,
And this life made a living Hell.

For I did naught in the way of perfecting,
Or making "worthy" this broken vessel...

But only Cried out for Love, Unconditional.

And if that Love without condition had not come,
Simply because I Am...

I would surely have Cried myself to death.

BECAUSE AND NOT BECAUSE

There is love,
And there is...
Love.

One arises from a subject,
And is given to an object,
In response to conditionality.

The other, being subjectless,
Knows no object,
And yet... Blesses all.

One is bundled,
With a thousand desires,
And arises "because of".

The other, Full and Complete,
Shines simply because…
It is Its nature.

The Lover, full of Longing,
Desires to hold The Beloved,
For all Eternity.

Only to find,
In the instant of touching…
That Lover, Beloved, and Time Vanish…

And only Love remains.

SO GENTLY

How many ages I wandered,
How many lifetimes,
In search of the Beloved.

Following the Fragrance,
I wandered for Eternities,
Until I could wander no more.

And there… exhausted,
Collapsed in despair, falling,
Into the Depths of my own Heart.

Where, beyond all hope,
My tear-stained face was lifted,
So gently…

LOVE ALONE IS MY COUNSEL

Of the teachers in my long life,
One proved Fruitful above all others;
The Unquenchable Longing,
Of Love's Ember, Glimmering,
In my Heart's deepest Interiority.

It was into and as that Flame,
The formless Essence of my Being,
That teacher and student Vanished,
And there, before duality ever was,
Only Causeless Love remained.

Not a Buddhist, this teacher,
Not a Hindu, this guru,
Not a Muslim, this murshid,
Not a Christian, this priest,
Yet… all of these, and more.

For Love, alone, is my Counsel.

LOVE SHINES

Love Shines,
In the Wellspring of the Heart,
For no one or anything in particular.

Transcendent,
It is simply the nature, inherent,
Of the Essence of Being.

And yet…
Everything and everyone,
Is Lit by its Grace.

Immanence,
The Compassionate Flow of Grace,
Into manifest Creation.

This is how the Flame in one Heart,
Ignites, through its Light and Warmth,
The Ember in another.

YOU'RE DRIVING

You're driving, not me.
It's all up to you, my friend,
How long we travel together,
Along this ancient road.

In the Garden of the Beloved

I'm an Idiot,
And have long since forgotten,
Where I'm going,
Or why.

Pulling over, you asked,
"What's this I Feel"?!
And so I got in to explain,
That I haven't a clue.

As long as you're satisfied with that,
And don't mind simply... driving,
I will ride with you,
Cruisin', the Wind of Eternity in our hair.

I Loved when you turned and said,
With Happiness, not regret,
"Now I'm not getting anywhere"!
And we laughed for miles.

Two Idiots now, not one.
Both found at last,
And utterly Lost.
Road tripping into the Unknown.

It's up to you how far we travel,
Together down this road,
Ever appearing, ever vanishing.
You're driving, not me.

You can drop me off anytime,
And we will be friends as we were,
When you first pulled over and asked,
"What's this I Feel"?!

"What's this"?!
I haven't a clue.
What, where, why, how?
We're not getting anywhere.

What an Unimaginable Blessing.

THE VILLAGE GATE

The author apologizes for using words,
For speaking dualistically one moment,
And absolutely the next;
For taking the transcendent view breathing in,
And the immanent view breathing out.

The mind is uneasy in confusion,
But the Heart reads chaos as poetry.

The mind lives within the walled village,
Of knowledge and ordered reason.
The Heart wanders far from "civilization",
In the Wilderness of the Great Mystery.

In the Garden of the Beloved

Reasoning can bring one to the village gates,
But only the Heart will push them open,
And move us out, into the Unknowable,
Out, into the Inexpressible.

There, a mind not yet ready, shudders,
And quickly builds a new village.
But a mind Blessed by Grace stands naked,
Illumined by the Vastness of Unknowing.

There, an unfortunate heart succumbs to fear,
And falls down quaking,
But a Heart Blessed by Grace surrenders,
To Unbearable, Crushing Wonder.

Longing is Grace,
Love is Grace,
Beauty is Grace,
Richness of Heart is Grace.

Push open the village gate.

Until, upon a path grown pathless,
Heart and Mind, Heaven and Earth,
Vanish like an ephemeral mist,
Into and as The Great Mystery.

MUST I KNOW?

"I know nothing.
I understand nothing.
I am unaware of Myself.
I am in Love, but with whom I do not know".

-Farid ud-Din Attar

It's a Mystery.
I don't know anything,
About anything,
Whatsoever.

Is that OK?

Must I know,
The what, when, and how,
The why and wherefore?
Need I be confident, assured,
And speak with authority?

Do you really want to hear,
More words "about"…
More descriptions "of"…
Or can we simply sit,
In this Radiance...

And Breathe Bliss.

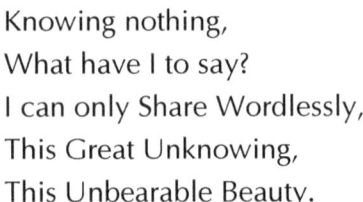 In the Garden of the Beloved

Knowing nothing,
What have I to say?
I can only Share Wordlessly,
This Great Unknowing,
This Unbearable Beauty.

But at the risk of knowing one thing,
I will say this much:
This Ecstasy…
It's…
You,

What you Are,
Before creation appears to You,
Before "you" appear to You.
The Nature of…
Your Essence.

Fullness, Completion, and Bliss.

Oh, how uncomfortable,
To speak even that much,
As if I know anything,
Of anything,
Whatsoever.

Maybe, if I whisper…
Barely speaking…

It's…

You.

THE BRAMBLES OF EXPERIENCE

Rummaging through the brambles of Experience in Form,
In search of sweet berries,
I emerge, scratched and bleeding,
Over and over again.

The Mother of Creation struggles to hold me, feigning severity,
As I squirm and giggle.

Laughing away Her chiding, wincing in pain, I exclaim,
"Oh Mother! How I love those berries"!

She relents her fierceness, laughs, and holds my face,
Tenderly wiping the sorrow-stained tears of Joy.

"I know, My Love.
I made their delight, and their sorrow, just for you.

They bring you always…

Back to Me".

FARAWAY HEAVEN

I confess that returning from Heaven,
The whole of my Being, reborn,
Sighed and moaned in The Primal Pain,
Of individuated existence.

Having existed as That which Remained,
When "I" and the world Vanished,
Returning to form, as "I" once again,
Was the Anguish of all Anguishes.

And if The Beautiful One, The Beloved,
Had not inhabited my Heart, thereafter,
I would surely have cried myself to death,
Having lost the Eden all Hearts desire.

But The Merciful Thief of all Sorrows,
In the greatest of Kindnesses,
Stole from me, and hid, any desire,
For return to that Faraway Heaven.

And in its place, Gifted this vagrant,
With a Tavern at the Heart of Being,
Where Drunkenness removes all desire,
Of anything greater than This…

For Faraway Heaven is Here.

BEFORE THE DREAM OF DUALITIES

Creation is the kingdom of dualities,
And the ever changing weather,
Of opposites ebbing and flowing,
One moment brightened and sunlit,
Another, darkening with clouds,
And we, either dancing or sheltering.

But within us, I swear, is an Essence,
A placeless Place, a timeless Time,
Where we Exist as That which Exists,
Before the birth of manifest creation,
And ourself, alive, existing within it;
The Kingdom of Heaven, within.

Neither the corruptions of religion,
Born of men, inflicted at their hands,
Nor the vicissitudes of philosophies,
Can wither the Rose in that Garden,
Or make vinegar of the Sweet Wine,
Served at The Tavern of The Beloved,
Where, before the Dream of dualities…

Lover and Beloved are One.

WHEN ONLY HEAVEN REMAINS

What we are, conceptually, is one thing,
Best left to philosophers and theologians;
What we are, Experientially, is quite another.

For we can gain profound understanding,
Of the birth and nature of outer reality,
Yet suffer within, not Knowing ourself.

Those investigating the nature of the outer,
Create systems, cosmologies, theologies,
Saying, "If this, then that, then surely thus."

Those investigating the nature of the Inner,
Uncreate systems, cosmologies, theologies,
And all that has accrued, over time, as "me".

One way increases, from more to ever more,
The other Diminishes, from less to ever less,
Until the "I" in "I Am" is no more…

And only Heaven Remains.

THE RIVER OF GRACE

For so very long, the river sought the Ocean,
Moved by a powerful current of Longing,
Encountering obstacles along the way,
Eddying, then flowing, ebbing then flowing,
But moving, relentlessly, unstoppable.

The river arrived, at last, at the Vastness,
And the waters merged, indistinguishable,
In the Fathomless Ecstasy of Union,
The river Vanishing, the Ocean Remaining,
Until, impossibly, yet another miracle occurred.

For the Indivisible Ocean flowed, through Grace,
Upstream, into the river of individuation,
The fresh water of selfhood, becoming Salted,
The current of the river's Longing, slowed,
Then halted, in Peace and Fulfillment.

How is it possible for the Salt of our Essence,
To exist within these individuated waters,
Where Beloved Ocean and Lover River swirl,
In a Dance of Inexpressible Sublimity,
And individuation loses all meaning?

The River of Grace.

HUH? WHAT? SHHHH!

It's my job, my duty, said the mind,
To investigate and ascertain,
The nature of this Mystery,
Of embodied existence,
In the dream of space and time.

After all, someone has to learn,
The twists, turns, and pitfalls,
Of this long and winding road,
So that heart, mind, and Soul,
Can move safely through this life.

This manifest form is fading now,
And I can say with humble pride,
That I have navigated we three,
Through countless joys and sorrows,
Through gains, loss, and doldrums.

In the Garden of the Beloved

But in all these many long years,
I've learned little to nothing at all,
Of the Mystery of our existence,
And have, in the end, acquired only,
A library of theory and conjecture.

And when I turn and ask The Heart,
What She thinks of my conundrum,
She seems not to have heard me,
Lost in Reverie of The Beloved,
But turns at last, whispering dreamily…

"Huh? What? Shhhh!"

IN CLOSING

All of these words I have written about Liberation, and Illumination,
May have given you the illusion that I have my bearings,
And an understanding of all that's unfolded,
And all that is to unfold in time,
When I am simply adrift,
Without compass,

Rudderless,

Here…

In this Great Mystery.

For the most comprehensive and up-to-date collection
of poems, visit https://GardenOfTheBeloved.com.

www.ingramcontent.com/pod-product-compliance
Lightning Source LLC
Chambersburg PA
CBHW051256120626
46547CB00015B/1962